0 00 01 1489. W9-BSV-196

Quintessential Guide to Using Consultants

David Zahn

HRD Press, Inc. • Amherst • Massachusetts

Published by: HRD Press, Inc.
                22 Amherst Road
                Amherst, MA 01002
                (800) 822-2801 (U.S. and Canada)
                (413) 253-3488
                (413) 253-3490 (Fax)
                http://www.hrdpress.com

Copyright © 2004 by HRD Press, Inc.

All rights reserved under International and Pan-American Copyright
Conventions. No part of this book may be reproduced in any form
or by any means, electronic or mechanical, including photocopying,
without permission in writing from the publisher. All inquiries
should be addressed to HRD Press, Inc., 22 Amherst Road,
Amherst, Massachusetts 01002. Published in the United States
by HRD Press, Inc.

ISBN 0-87425-794-8

Typesetting by Pracharak Technologies (P) Ltd., Madras, India
Cover design by Eileen Klockars
Editorial work by Sally Farnham

Contents

Dedication

This book is dedicated to the memory of my first, and best consultant, my father, Fred Zahn.

Acknowledgments

Any time a project of this magnitude is undertaken, there are many people that contribute to its success and give of themselves selflessly because they believe in the content, the person driving it, or have a un-obscured vision of the book's potential that even the author sometimes can't see. This book is built on the contributions of many such people. My literary agent, Danielle Jatlow of Waterside Productions, Inc. offered gentle encouragement and a steadying influence when the idea for this book was first blossoming. The fine folks of HRD Press deserve my gratitude (and I hope yours once you finish reading this book) for agreeing that this topic deserved a spot in their portfolio of books. They are truly professionals and have been a pleasure to work with on this project. The clients, consultants, peers, subordinates, and supervisors I have met along the way have all helped to shape the text within this book. Some by adding insights, some by demonstrating what NOT to do, and others by sharing the journey along the way that has included many late nights, too many deadlines to count, and the pleasures and pains of making a living out of a suitcase running to catch the next flight. Finally, my business partner Jeff Clow who believed in me and what I had to offer to the world of consulting when I was still in my 20's, and has never wavered in that belief. He has provided a sounding board, instruction, motivation, and a friendship that knows no bounds. Much of what is distilled in this book is the result of lunches consumed with Jeff; laughing, bemoaning, comparing ideas, debating, and all the while being careful not to squeeze the ketchup packets too forcefully and splattering each other. He truly is my brother-in-arms in this endeavor and for that I am grateful.

About the Author

David Zahn is a Managing Partner in Clow Zahn Associates, LLC, a sales consultancy primarily focused on addressing the sales and sales support issues of the Consumer Packaged Goods industry. Their roster of clients include such recognizable names as; Dr Pepper/7UP, ConAgra, Tropicana, United Distillers and Vintners, Dreyer's, among others. David's academic preparation and background in Instructional Design, as well as his experience with training over 10,000 client attendees during his 17 year career has provided him with a unique and insightful perspective on what differentiates a quality consulting engagement from a less successful one. A frequent contributor to radio interview shows, industry publications, webzines, and other journals and periodicals addressing both consulting issues and sales specific issues, David is also the author of "How to be a Successful Independent Consultant, Fourth Edition" which he co-authored with Herman Holtz. When not engaged with clients, writing or presenting at industry meetings, David can usually be found with his children, Brian and Michael, eating Buffalo chicken wings, or watching them play soccer.

Why I Wrote This Book

If you are reading this book, you are in one of two camps: Either you are a business person considering using a consultant and looking for guidance on how best to do that, or you are a consultant trying to understand "the other side" so that you can better accomplish your goals. While this book is written from the perspective of what a client or prospective client often confronts when deciding to use a consultant, there are ample examples of how successful consultants think, act, and behave to benefit the reader hoping to gain an advantage over his or her competition within the consulting ranks. In either case, it is my intention to provide enough kernels of insights and nuggets of practical hints within these pages to meet your needs.

In today's corporate environment, employees are being asked to work faster, harder, and in a more technologically integrated way, and to accomplish more with fewer resources. Additionally, the scope of jobs has changed dramatically, and the specialization required of corporate employees to achieve results has increased exponentially. There is also less time and patience for people to "grow into" their jobs and learn through their own experiences. Factor into this environment of frenzied activity an economy that demands excellent execution the first time and every time, causing managers to have to increasingly rely on the expertise and experience of outside suppliers, vendors, and consultants.

More and more projects are being "outsourced," and it is becoming more acceptable and common for employees to "manage vendors" on projects that require unique areas of expertise or experience. The skills necessary to properly shepherd a project and the relationship with the consultant through to a successful conclusion need to be addressed and provided for corporate employees asked to perform under these oftentimes unfamiliar conditions. This book will fill the void left by corporations demanding competence of employees assigned to use consultants judiciously without being provided the necessary developmental opportunities, exposures, and experiences.

There are many helpful resources available, such as books, videos, and training workshops, that address managing internal employees. But using a consultant hired only to complete a specific project requires a managerial skill set that is separate and unique from that used with internal full-time employees. This book is designed to fill that skill vacuum and provide the person managing the relationship with the consultant with the necessary insight, support, and guidance to ensure a more productive (and pleasant) outcome through the use of outside experts.

This book will explain these skills, put them into the context of real-world applications, and provide guidance and advice on how to maximize the results of the consulting relationship through each step of the process. It is intended mainly for those internal employees who need to broaden their experience to include successfully working with consultants. In addition, this book will be a resource for corporate managers and executives that provides the same level of guidance and direction available to the consultants who call upon them.

With the economy's recent downturn, corporations now have many more consulting options. Many former employees of a particular company have "opened shop" as consultants either as a way to earn income as they await their next corporate assignment, or as a tentative approach to entering and sampling a new career, or even as a full-time endeavor that they are committed to as a chosen occupation. One of my goals in writing this book is help the reader sift out when it is wise to rely on a former colleague with "inside knowledge" of their company's policies, procedures, customers, processes, etc., and when it is better to use an expert who is not "home-grown."

One of the major motivators that compelled me to write this book was a desire to improve upon the results of completed consulting projects. It has been my experience and the experience of many of the clients, professionals, and even a few "hacks" who I have worked with over the years that projects conceived under the best of intentions all too often are "delivered as stillborns" by the conclusion of the project. Upon the project failing to achieve all that was intended, the inevitable finger-pointing, finding-fault, determining-culpability, and assigning-blame exercises begin. The truth is that in the consulting business, the client always has the upper-hand because the client votes with the checkbook and the consultant all too often is governed by the power of currency over sage counsel or advice. But no matter which side is ultimately seen as being at fault, the relationship between the consultant and client, and perhaps all subsequent relationships between future clients and consultants, will forever be sullied by a project that went bad.

This book is my contribution to the field in providing a healthy dose of preventative medicine, pre-natal care for unborn consulting projects, marital counseling to clients and consultants considering relationships, and some common-sense child-rearing advice for projects as they develop and mature. It is my hope that through some exploration of the issues that commonly derail otherwise well-intentioned projects and the investigation of those practices that facilitate successful consulting initiatives, that more consulting projects will lead to positive outcomes. In addition, the sometimes cynical view taken toward aspects of consulting as a practice and a profession can be softened through the building of awareness provided in this book and the implementation of the suggestions included in the following chapters.

Lastly, it is my intention to spread with "evangelical zeal" the best practices gleaned from my own perspectives from both sides of the relationship and reveal the scars, bruises, and thick skin earned during a career that has been dedicated to working with clients as a consultant, and with consultants as a client. Consultants reading this book will agree that clients can be lumped into different categories: those who know exactly what they want and how they wish to receive the help; those who only think they know, but are wrong; those who know, but don't want to hear it; and those who don't know at all and are hoping to shift responsibility or blame for their ignorance to others who can be hired as consultants, only to then be fired to demonstrate what a person of action and "bottom-line orientation" they hope to delude the client organization into thinking they are. I offer you the wisdom reaped from all these sources, but provide you with the proviso that the learning on which this book is founded is not complete. I continue to learn from my own experiences, my clients' sharing of their experiences with other consultants, my competitors' constant forcing of me to re-assess and evaluate my approaches and techniques, and my peers' continuous goading of me to improve that which I was unaware needed addressing.

I will consider this book a success if it helps close the yawning gap in the business literature focused on the *client* perspective on consulting relationships. While there is much written on topics of interest to the consultant reader that are as broad as general business or operational techniques, running your own business, financial insights for the service professional, etc., and then more specific tomes on approaching clients, managing client relationships, and maximizing impact with clients, etc., there is little available to assist the client seeking guidance on how best to approach consultants. To be sure, the consultant devotes large blocks of time to thinking about, chasing, and delivering business and therefore has a core need for the advice provided—or purported to be provided—in these books. Furthermore, a walk through any public library or a perusal of the shelves of a well-stocked bookstore (including the Internet versions) will quickly point out the plethora of information directed at and available to those who wish to become consultants, fancy themselves as consulting suppliers, or have ongoing viable careers as consulting providers or vendors. The titles entice the consultant-wanna-be's with strategies, processes, methods, and how-to guides that promise inner peace and joy, or at least the modern equivalent: a high-paying job with autonomy, excitement, creativity, and a chance to truly make a difference in the clients with whom one works.

Now, there obviously are some good books available that do promote ethical, appropriate, and business-relevant practices and do adhere to standards of engagement that are above reproach; however, I keep waiting to see some of the lesser-quality books retitled with names such as *How to Be a Consulting Parasite While Increasing Your Project Fees, Becoming Indispensable to Your Clients While Reducing Your Value, Be Successful or Be Gone,* etc. Many of these books seem to view the client as a necessary evil to be endured on the way to consulting nirvana, and it is my intention to provide the antidote to clients and prospects so that they are not "infected" by the misdirected, ill-informed, or even mal-intentioned consultants looking to prey upon unsuspecting clients. I can provide a little forewarning and preparation, and help the reader avoid a sticky and costly cure after a project has ended poorly.

Now compare the volume of work available to the consultant to what is available to the client/potential client. The corporate manager considering the use of consultants has a job that is not focused *solely* on the selection, management, and evaluation of consultants. This person is tasked with a particular role or function within the company and has likely become an expert in that discipline. While there are books addressing their area of expertise, there is precious little they can turn to or rely upon for assurances on how to navigate through the consulting choices available.

Therefore, this book is presented as a crutch for the uninitiated, a checklist for the experienced client, and a salve for the clients who have previously felt burned by consultants or consulting services, but are ready to try to do it better the next time. The sections of this book that most closely mirror the needs of the client organization or the reader, or represent the stage of the relationship with a consultant that is currently underway, will hopefully provide significant value. It is also my intention that this book be shared with the consultant chosen by the client. I can actually envision a prospect or client sitting down with a consultant and using this book to establish guidelines for their working relationship. As such, there is nothing secretive or confidential in what is contained within these pages. I have set out to provide approaches that are designed to benefit both the consultant and the client, and are not designed to give unfair advantage to one by "sneaking something past" the other or using leverage in an unethical manner.

Who This Book Is Meant For

The target audience for this book is, therefore, anyone and everyone who participates in the consulting relationship (client contact, client senior management, subject-matter expert assigned to work with a consultant, or consultant). Those who will derive maximum benefit from the techniques suggested are primarily:

1. Corporate employees considering or tasked with using consultants or others outside the direct employ of the company. Functionally, these employees might reside in Marketing, Sales, Human Resources, Information Technology, Manufacturing, Strategic Planning, or any other department within a company. Titles of the targeted reader/intended audience range from senior or executive management (VP or above) down through the corporate hierarchy to director- or manager-level employees.
2. Any and all industries and all sized companies. Generally speaking, this book is not industry specific, and the recommendations in it can be widely applied (the only exception is if the company does *not* use consultants or other experts such as accountants, attorneys, etc.).

Those readers who are in corporate environments and are considering the use of consultants will find value in the sections focused on:

- Determining the appropriate situations to use external consultants
- How to select a consultant
- Ways to contract with a consultant
- How to manage a consultant during the "life" of the project
- How to work *with* and not *against* a consultant
- Evaluating the work of a consultant
- Exiting the consulting relationship

Others who this book is targeted toward and who will find value in these pages are:

1. Consultants looking to strengthen their own approaches to (existing and potential) clients
2. Academics responsible for teaching courses on the consulting process or students in graduate-level institutions of management

Introduction— What Is a Consultant?

Key Learning Points:

- Defining what a consultant "is" and what one "does"
- Where to find a consultant
- What traits in common do consultants usually possess

---

consultant (1) *one who takes something you already know and makes it sound confusing* (2) *a colleague called in at the last second to share the blame*

Defining Consultant

The definition of a consultant according to *Webster's New Collegiate Dictionary* (1979) is (1) one who consults with another (2) one who gives professional advice or services: expert. According to *The American Heritage College Dictionary, Third Edition* (1993), a consultant is one that gives expert or professional advice, or one that consults another. Left to be determined then is what constitutes "expert" and what "professional" consists of in order for us to recognize if one is truly to be labeled a "consultant" according to the definition. A dictionary review of the meaning of "expert" leads us to understand that an expert is one who has a high degree of skill in or knowledge of a certain subject, or one who has mastered or achieved the highest level of competence through experience or training. The definition of "professional" is somewhat more nebulous and non-specific in helping us understand what a consultant is or does. *The American Heritage College Dictionary, Third Edition* (1993) provides multiple definitions that serve more to confuse than enlighten. Among the definitions offered are (1a) of, relating to, engaged in, or suitable for a profession, (1b) conforming to the standards of a profession, (2) engaging in a given activity as a source of livelihood or as a career, (3) performed by persons receiving pay, (4) having or showing great skill: expert. *The Webster's New Collegiate Dictionary* adds the following to the definition discussion of "professional": "characterized by or conforming to the technical or ethical standards of a profession" and then further includes "participating for gain or livelihood in an activity or field of endeavor often engaged in by amateurs."

To be fair, there are many practitioners of advice who do conform to standards of ethical interactions with others and are truly self-governed by codes of conduct that forbid nefarious or underhanded practices to take advantage of a client's need or ignorance. However, interpreting these terms is truly subjective. To date, there are precious few people making their livelihood as "consultants" who are "licensed" as consultants (in part due to the debates within the consulting community as to what standards to use, who determines or evaluates another's competence, whether there should be a "consulting" standard or just a "technical knowledge" standard, etc.). Furthermore, to define what a professional is *solely* on the basis of receiving compensation for services rendered that otherwise could have been provided by amateurs (and all that the word connotes) does little to separate the inherent value in what is being provided by the "consultant." In some instances, this might be an earned and deserved slight and is an accurate portrayal of what certain members of the consulting fraternities and sororities are offering to clients as services rendered. However, until there is universal agreement on what constitutes "good consulting practice" and what the criteria are for being able to consider one worthy of the title "consultant," marketplace dynamics will have to separate out those who are charlatans and unworthy of engagement from those who are aligned with the ethical, technical, and project requirements of clients and prospects. Having no governing body to determine standards and practices that all consultants should be required to adhere to means that clients must work that much harder to ensure that they are aware of the person, products, services, and expectations/promises when they agree to pay for what is in some instances "self-proclaimed expertise" by the consultant selling services to them. In few other economic transactions would people willingly spend money for an outcome for which they do not have a clear vision, be unsure of what the final result will be, and often base the decision on little more than "faith" and "belief" in the consultant to provide what they cannot provide to themselves.

Most business people and academics consider a consultant to be someone who is perceived to have "walked in my shoes" and can therefore provide advice or counsel that is likely to be imbued with the learning and best practices that can only be provided by a career spent addressing the very issues that are currently being asked to be addressed. Consultants' expertise is built on having done it themselves, perhaps studied it, and witnessed and/or contributed to others successfully addressing particular issues. The professionalism a consultant is expected to exhibit is of a standard that approaches being above reproach. This is often a major conflict that arises between clients and paid advice givers: The paid service provider often has to balance what is right for the client in the short and long term with what is right in the short and long term for themselves. How they make that decision can often lead to conflict, mistrust, and doubt as to their motivations by clients.

Anyone reading this far into this book has surely heard some of the jokes about what a consultant is, does, etc., and might have even relayed a few of them to a colleague to share a laugh. The bitterness left on the tongue (and wallet) of a client after a consulting assignment has gone awry can certainly fuel the cynicism and sarcasm that many of these jokes include. Casting aspersions on the consulting industry has become almost a cottage industry unto itself with almost every executive having had an experience that still causes nightmares and demands to be shared with others. While I do not wish to be an apologist for those who are not worthy of an apology within the consulting ranks, I do think that some projects that go over-budget, deliver poor results, and lead to less-than-satisfactory feelings about the experience are as much the responsibility of the client as the consultant.

A consultant is a business person with the same concerns and challenges as any other business person. The consultant worries about cash flow, staffing, new product/service development, managing expenses, revenue generation, etc. As a business person, the consultant often has to navigate the same seas as the client: economic downturns, competition, price pressures, managing vendors, and opening new accounts. The client's need for objective and oftentimes cost-effective counsel can be diametrically opposed to the consultant's own pressures and desire to "get what I can, while I can from this client." While this is unethical behavior and will ultimately prove the undoing of any practitioner of this business approach, pretending it does not happen or does not exist is naïve. The ability to provide objective counsel regardless of the consultant's own need is the sign of a true consulting professional—but it is not always as easy to provide as one would expect. After reading this book and applying the principles and techniques included within it on subsequent consulting projects, clients will see fewer incidences of hiring the wrong consultant for the wrong job and anticipating the wrong outcome, both consultants and clients will come to respect each other and possibly even enjoy the experience as one that is mutually enriching and productive.

What a Consultant Is and Is Not

A consultant is someone who has been hired to offer services for a fee based on the perceived (and one hopes, actual) level of competence at the task for which that consultant has been hired. Unlike an employee, the consultant is hired with the understanding that the contract is for a specific term or length of time, or until the achievement of a particular outcome (until the project is completed, for example). The agreement struck between consultant and client is that when the project has been concluded or the contracted length of time has been reached, the consultant will cease to be paid, and the client will no longer receive the benefit of having the consultant's services. The consultant might work temporarily in-house for the client or might never step foot in the client's office.* The consultant might be "at the service" of multiple employees or executives, or might be dedicated to assisting just one person or department/function. The client might wish to view and treat the consultant as if he or she were part of the "team," or the client might decide that the consultant is little more than "hired help" and would barely go to the effort to learn the consultant's name. The expectations for how much time the relationship will require, what output or results are to be expected, and what each will provide to the other in support of the project are all subject to agreement and negotiation.

However, at the root of the arrangement is that the consultant is to fulfill a contractual commitment that is of a specific duration and then all obligations between the parties shall cease. How specific that contract is and what is to be included in that agreement are the subject of much of the information to follow in this book.

It might also be advantageous to look at what a consultant *is not*. A consultant is not responsible for a client's mistakes or previous poor decisions. Hiring a consultant to hide or reverse historical results will end in frustration for both parties. A consultant is *not* responsible for a client's results: Never has been, and never will be. It is the responsibility of management to manage the business, and it is the charge of the consultant to advise, direct, enlighten, and provide guidance to management. Ultimately, it is management's role to decide and determine courses of action. There cannot be confusion around this point. Consultants do *not* run their clients' businesses for them. Just as a school teacher is responsible for covering the mandated curriculum, but not for taking tests for students to judge the class's mastery of

---

*The Internal Revenue Service has various criteria for determining when someone is a "vendor" or "supplier" of services and when one should be considered an "employee." This difference in part hinges on where the work is done; however, a consultant does not *necessarily* need to work out of their own facilities at all times to still be considered a vendor or supplier and not a consultant. For the most current rulings and interpretations on this and other legal matters, it is *strongly* required that specific legal and accounting counsel be sought.

the subject taught, a consultant is not expected to sit in the CEO's seat (or other executive's seat) and make decisions for the client. This point will be addressed again when we discuss whether it makes sense to include client results as part of the compensation structure for a consultant's efforts. For now, as emphatically as can be stated, consultants are not well suited for "Father confessor" roles, for assuming responsibility for a client's efforts, or for playing scapegoat for poor management decisions (that is, hired so that they can be blamed and fired in a demonstration of management strength).

Consulting both benefits from and is hindered by the economical realities that it operates within. For someone to refer to him- or herself as a consultant requires little more than a business card and the audacity to try to acquire business from a client willing to pay for services rendered (and the business card is optional). Because there are no formal standards that are *absolutes* in achieving the title or rank of "consultant," it is a career option that is available to anybody at any particular point in their own career development. The image that some have of an avuncular figure who is the "voice of wisdom" based on years of experience and a series of successfully more complex professional assignments does not always fit the reality of those who call themselves a "consultant." The consulting ranks include part-timers, those seeking income temporarily as they transition between jobs, and those who are ill-suited to work for others and establish their own businesses based on technical or professional skills. Consultants might work out of their bedrooms or on their kitchen tables, or might be part of much larger monolithic organizations, and everything in between—including loose "networks" of consultants who align with one another on projects where it makes sense to do so, and operate independently of one another at other times. The "cost of entry" into the field of consulting poses no real hurdle to anyone with a skill or talent that some client might value and be willing to pay for.

The good news is that anyone who wants to be a consultant, can be a consultant. The bad news is also that anyone who wants to be a consultant, can be a consultant. Being able to decipher which consultants are worth their fees and which are not becomes a puzzling mix of "gut intuition" and "objective comparisons" that are as often as individual as the person making that decision.

In general, the number of consultants swells at the polar ends of the continuum of business cycles. When businesses are doing well, they are more apt to want to spend money on new, innovative approaches, improve their current market positions, and facilitate employee and machinery upgrades. At the other end of the business cycle, when businesses are hurting, they are more prone to feel they *need* to spend out of desperation to sustain or save their current market position or to fend off a competitor's advantage. In both cases, service providers fill the void and seek to meet the needs of those companies. Consultants, or would-be consultants, meet the need either through moonlighting from their current full-time jobs, taking the "leap" into self-employment, aligning with an existing consulting firm, or in the instance of bad economic times, needing to generate income to sustain their lifestyle after being laid off or having their employment terminated.

The time when consulting languishes is when there is movement toward the middle of the economic cycles and businesses are holding their own in general, but there is little perceived need to change. One recent example of this phenomenon is the recent so-called "Dot. bomb" fiascoes. As the economy was gearing up and seeming to change in accordance with the "Internet economy," there was a huge wave of consultants who sprung up to meet the need head-on: consultants in HTML code and Web design, consultants in market research and consumer demographics, consultants in logistics to convert business models of "brick and mortar" stores to "virtual" stores, etc. As all of us have now come to realize, there were inherent weaknesses in basing an economy that was not transaction based, but was predicated on "eyeballs" and "exposures." How many successful shopkeepers track and evaluate window shoppers as more desirable than actual purchasers?

In a strange turn of events, I had been asked by a director of training at one of the better-known Internet shopping sites to propose how to train store-level clerks to properly process and use a "discount card" that was available to shoppers who had pre-registered for the card online. In the time it took to generate a proposal and present it back to the prospect/client (approximately one week), the Internet site had been shut down and all the employees had been given their "walking papers." In a strange twist of fate, my contact for that project on the client side then called me and inquired about my interest in having her work for my firm as an expert consultant on "failed Internet companies and what employees can do to protect themselves." I passed on that opportunity because my fear was that the answer was going to be to make friends with me and await a job offer to join my firm. However, I share that anecdote because it does represent how fluid and dynamic the economy is in creating consulting opportunities in the best of times (when the economy seemed to be leaning in the direction that all that is Internet is good) and when it crashed (and now our consulting practice was viewed as a stable place to work and counsel others on how to avoid the mistakes that this former employee had made). If nothing else, the Dot.com balloon deflating certainly brought into sharp focus the alacrity with which consultants can rise to meet needs on the way up, and also on the way down as on both sides of that experience, consultants (some well positioned to offer counsel, and others more opportunistic and a whole lot less deserved) conferred, advised, and counseled business leaders through the maze of blind alleys and mirages of opportunities.

Where to Find Consultants

Industry pundits have estimated that the consulting industry generates between 30 billion and 100 billion U.S. dollars in project fees (the disparity is mostly a result of determining what exactly qualifies as a consulting project and what is categorized as something else). Of this business, the major players tend to get only a small percentage of the total business (according to a recently published newsletter from SAP INFO, No. 90, published in 2002 and available electronically at www. sapinfo.net), with the overwhelming majority of the business going to mid-tier and smaller players with a specific focus or unique insight into particular technology or industry issues.

Consultants and consulting organizations are as varied and different as the assignments they pursue. Consultants can at times "flock" together in organizations that are focused and dedicated to consulting as a business pursuit with hierarchical structures and management policies in place to ensure the ongoing maintenance of revenue from existing clients, chase new projects from existing clients or prospects, and manage fiscal responsibilities inherent in running a business that has "intellectual capital" as its primary product. Examples of firms primarily focused on providing consultation are Boston Consulting Group, McKinsey & Company, and Towers Perrin.

Other firms view consulting as a strong "value-added" service they can provide, but consider it supplemental to the mission or purpose of the company. As of recent business ethics interest and of historical note, companies that have used this business model have had to address how to maintain the business objectivity required to offer counsel and advice that is genuinely in the best interest of the client organization and, at the same time, remain focused on the internal business realities that they confront in building synergies with sister divisions of their parent company. Much of the hue and cry that has confronted the larger accounting firms with consulting divisions and the larger technology providers that also provide either general business advice or even very function- or task-specific consulting is how to separate the need to serve "two masters" (the client and at the same time a parent company searching for revenue opportunities within a receptive client organization that might be able to be led to a solution that is not in their own best interests, but satisfies the needs of the consulting organization to expand their "reach" into clients). There are several companies that have had to address this issue and have been in the news as of late (some for positive approaches and, unfortunately, some others for less-than-positive outcomes). Arthur Andersen first made headlines by splitting off from the original company and creating the Accenture Consulting Company. The whole of Arthur Andersen then crumbled in the wake of the Enron scandal. Companies that have recently been tracked by the business press for innovatively trying to acquire and then meld (if not merge) the core business practice with the newly incorporated consulting division are IBM and their PriceWaterhouseCoopers (PwC) Division, and Ernst & Young becoming part of Cap Gemini.

On the other hand, some consulting firms have remained vigilant in not wanting to align with any particular accounting or technology business because of the impact it might have on the quality, or perceived quality, of advice provided. One of the best examples of this is the longstanding view by McKinsey & Company (going back to Marvin Bowers who replaced James McKinsey as the leader of McKinsey) that accounting and consulting cannot reside under the same roof without leading to conflict and issues in objective counsel given the inherent cross purposes that those two initiatives often serve.

Mid-tier consulting firms tend to be "industry vertical" or "function specific" in orientation. Because these consultants tend to be experts from the industry that client organizations currently compete within, they don't typically focus on larger strategic issues that incorporate the entirety of the client's organization to implement a recommended solution, or target across multiple industry client prospects. These consultants tend to remain focused on one industry. They might further narrow their consulting expertise to functions or departments, or they may choose to cross industries, but remain focused on a small number of departments or functions. Examples include certain firms that specialize in Customer Relationship Management or CRM; human resources firms that are strong in Benefits and Administration, but also have employee selection or training consulting strength; and various information technology firms that can provide assistance in real-time processing of remotely collected data, but can also assist in Web design and/or payment-tracking information. These firms straddle between the multi-million dollar and multi-year budgeted projects that the larger, more strategic consulting firms often pursue, and the shorter duration, less comprehensive, and smaller investment assignments that the "boutique" consulting operations typically target.

The last group of consultants are the so-called "boutique" consultants. These consultants tend to be smaller in scope and size and are rarely awarded projects that require the depth and breadth that the larger consulting firms can handle. However, they are often an integral part of the larger firms' project execution by sub-contracting for labor, expertise, or implementation support. A boutique firm might sell services directly to the end-user client, or might choose to provide consultative support to a larger consulting firm in the completion of a large-scale project. The difference in these two approaches is often reflected in the fees generated by the service provided and the level of involvement and complexity of the request. Many boutique shops do not have the "reach or touch" into the offices of clients making decisions that could benefit from their expertise due to lack of exposure, inability to sell, or other factors. Therefore, they rely on the larger firm to "sell" their services for them (oftentimes, anonymously), and they take a percentage of the total project fee in support of the larger firm's efforts.

Other "boutiques" are small (sometimes even just one person relying on personal contacts to generate sufficient business) and prefer to focus their attention to a small sphere of clients either geographically or within a limited number of industry or functional areas of insight. A former VP of Marketing, for example, might become a consultant who assists firms with consumer or demographic research, but limits the practice to only firms within driving distance from home, or perhaps works only with firms that sell pharmaceuticals or some other business segment. Whereas larger competitors are often slower to respond to changes in business due to their bigger infrastructure and size, the boutique can be more nimble and responsive to industry needs, but sacrifices the benefits of the larger firms' resources in exchange for the dexterity and flexibility that comes with being small enough to change direction rapidly.

An emerging service that consultants and clients have begun to take advantage of is that of the "consulting broker." These firms form relationships with clients seeking consulting services on the one hand, and consultants seeking engagements (pre-screened by the broker) on the other hand.

The pre-screening of the consultants includes a rigorous profile of their skills, background, and experience. This enables the broker to make a "best match" with clients seeking services. The consulting firms generally pay the broker a percentage of their engagement fee; other fees may also be included for the consulting firms.

Separate and distinct from the entities described above is the former employee who might have been temporarily laid off during an economic downturn, but still has a valuable contribution to make to the company. But instead of serving as an employee, this person will perform as a contractor. The expectation might be that the arrangement is temporary, but it still is a consulting arrangement for the duration of the project or projects. This consultant does not view this as a full-time, long-term pursuit and will likely have to decide if the arrangement is a viable alternative for generating income the longer it lasts.

Related to this temporary employee is the recently retired or moonlighting employee. Some people find themselves to be bored upon retirement or are seeking additional income to what they are earning in their current job. While they might enjoy the work or the income it produces, they do not view it as their primary means of generating income. It is supplemental at best. The work might represent a chance to "dabble" in an avocation or interest area to determine the viability of eventually pursuing it more diligently. While these people will "consult" in the strictest definition of the word by offering advisory services to meet business challenges, they tend to operate in very small universes, relying almost exclusively on personal contacts and referrals from friends and family.

Although these last two categories might not appear to be a large threat to consulting organizations that are chartered with the specific purpose of offering consulting services, they represent a large and undocumented percentage of the business that is outsourced by companies. The reasons are multi-fold and logical when examined:

- The person is often known and trusted by the client after having worked for the client for years and having always done good work.
- The fees are often less than a larger firm would charge. These people can factor less overhead into their pricing since they typically work on a kitchen table or in a spare bedroom. Or perhaps they are ignorant of what the "market for services" is, and they undercut it and get the business.
- Less time is needed to train or orient the consultant to the unique ways of the client company.
- The consultant often has the upper-hand over competitors because they know, or have access to people internally who know, when particular pieces of business or projects will be needed. Therefore, they can directly approach the decision-maker and pitch their business proposal prior to the job being put out to bid.

Consultants might congregate together to try to form larger and more comprehensive offerings to clients, or they might be more like a "lone wolf" seeking projects without the encumbrance of a larger entity and the inherent issues of working with or for other people. Regardless of where they are, though, they tend to have certain features in common.

Who Are Consultants?

As we saw in the previous section, consultants can approach their businesses very differently. Some of them are dedicated to the business or profession of advice giving, and some are looking for a way to tide them over until a full-time job comes along. Others who are retired and not quite ready to "get out of the game" might still seek the adventure and independence of working on projects. There are still others who are more focused on supplementing their income, but either are not emotionally ready, are not financially prepared, or do not possess enough ability to provide consulting services as their primary source of income.

With that said, identifying or profiling who is a consultant and who is not is no easy task. A consultant might be the software developer with a ponytail, earring, and tattoos; or the "technology whiz" wearing the prototypical pocket protector and working on developing a customized information services platform for a financial services firm; or the marketing executive wearing the Hermes scarf, Prada shoes, and Tiffany bracelet and developing a new product launch to coincide with a revamped advertising campaign. Identifying a consultant by appearance or "uniform" is a task that has a success rate that approaches randomness in accuracy. However, regardless of how consultants might look to the outside world, what is occurring on the inside, out of sight from the world, might begin to demonstrate just how similar these seemingly different-looking people are with one another.

Trait #1: Belief in the Monetary Value of Service/Product

First and foremost before a consultant can ever secure his or her first contract or assignment, there has to be a belief that he or she has something of monetary value to impart or provide. This obvious point becomes a very sticky issue later on when the consultant discusses such issues as pricing, management of projects, and responsibility for outcomes with potential clients. However, until a person believes that he or she can deliver something that another person will find worthwhile and is willing to pay for, there is no opportunity for that person to consult. Turning that idea on its head, until a client perceives that someone can provide a solution that has value to him or her, there is no consulting relationship. An undercurrent, then, in the relationship is that the consultant believes they have something that is desirable to another and that has a monetary value, and the prospect or client believes there is a need that can be met by an outsider and is willing to pay to have that need met.

Trait #2: Strong Sense of "Self"

Consulting is slightly different than other careers or professions in that it requires selling what is often unseen: a certain "result." The result is what is being purchased, and the client is sometimes unsure of how to get to the result or might have minimal interest in understanding how the result is derived, but knows that a particular result is desired. Therefore, unlike other jobs where the "inputs" and "outputs" of the work are clearly defined, a consultant is selling a vision of a better future (one that either contains less risk, pain, randomness, or other negative outcome, or a future that includes more accuracy, more efficiency, better controls, etc.).

In most sales situations, the buyer purchases a product that he or she knows and is familiar with. The buyer is aware of what the product can and cannot do, what need it fulfills, and even the approximate cost of the product. The salesperson's job in these instances is to appeal to the buyer's so-called "hot buttons" (image, affiliation, alignment, etc.). A consultant will similarly leverage "hot buttons," but will use those relevant to business (competitive pressures, promotion opportunity, reduction in time-to-market, etc.). The difference, though, is that a consultant in many instances sells him- or herself and what is between his or her ears, not something that comes in a box or is delivered off the back of a truck. There are times when there is not an example from a prior engagement to demonstrate to the prospect how something will "work" or a product to tangibly view and touch to explain the potential outcome to the client. All that the consultant can rely upon is his or her own credibility, earnestness, trustworthiness, and perceived competence in the eyes of the client. Any client who gets that gnawing feeling that they are being sold something the consultant can't deliver on is bound to eliminate that consultant from future consideration, as well they should. After all, it is the client contact who will have to live with the results and will be responsible for the repercussions of either a well-integrated and -executed solution, or one that fails to achieve what was intended and might in fact do harm.

For a consultant to succeed, an ability to convey confidence and success is desirable. No client or prospect wants to hire a consultant who does not believe they can accomplish the task, therefore a client should focus on how strongly the consultant believes he or she can resolve the assignment positively and how that consultant rises to challenges. In fact, an aware client will sort out consultants who hide behind a false bravado and confidence, and who actually exhibit fear due to their lack of experience.

Trait #3: Business Person First, Expert Second

A consultant is a business person first and foremost. The business that consultant is in is the expertise business, but the expert who does not know how to manage a business will cease to have opportunity to apply that expertise for clients. That person will quickly find themselves working for others who know how to run a business and can properly leverage the expertise of the wanna-be consultant. A businessperson must track and manage the needs of a business to sustain long-term viability. While the expert in sales processes might not enjoy learning or performing the required steps in accounting to properly apportion time and materials against projects, failure to do so will result in a poorly run business and ultimately the cessation of the consulting practice due to cash flow problems, billing issues, etc.

As a client, it is vital to understand that, while working with someone who is most likely experienced and chosen for their competence in addressing a particular business issue, this person must also be cognizant of factors that extend beyond the execution of that project and encroach upon issues like payment cycles, marketing, new product development, tax forms, etc. These elements might not directly impact the completion of the assigned project and certainly should not get in the way of success, but knowing that the consultant is juggling these factors behind the scenes might also help decipher behaviors and pressures that otherwise would not be apparent to a client.

A consultant who does not have good organizational skills is destined to lose out on many opportunities. The consultant must be comfortable working seamlessly with the client's internal subject-matter experts on one project, and then responding to a request from the Accounts Payable function on a recent invoice, or addressing a future project with a senior-level executive, all the while managing the consulting cycle of "Sell–Do." Consultants will very often fall into the trap of focusing their efforts on business acquisition in slow times, and then, once a few projects have been sold, they devote themselves to delivering on those projects and remove themselves from the selling chores, only to find that as those previously sold projects begin to wind down, they have to then gear up again to sell more projects to replace the ones that are concluding. A well-organized consultant will maintain a steady effort against both endeavors so that there is a leveling of the wild peaks and valleys of business that might otherwise occur and cause havoc with cash flow, project management, and scheduling.

Trait #4: Communicator
A consultant must be comfortable imparting his or her enthusiasm for a topic to another person and "infecting" that person (or at least spreading the zeal) with the same level of enthusiasm. However, as the saying goes, "All hat and no cattle, do not a cowboy make." The ability to sustain that enthusiasm throughout a project over much iteration, challenges, edits, and changes in direction requires someone who excels at communicating. A good consultant will update the client contact on the project's progress, identify obstacles as they appear, and continue to re-sell the project to each new person they meet within the client company as necessary (more on this topic in another chapter). As such, their communication skills must be finely honed so that they can provide the information needed in a palatable and digestible form for audiences that might be as disparate as the board of directors all the way to a part-time data entry clerk (depending on the project requirements, of course). Clients often test the consultant's communication ability by envisioning the consultant explaining the project and the perceived benefit of the initiative to peers, supervisors, and subordinates. If the consultant can successfully communicate the rationale for the project and the perceived benefits so that each audience comes away understanding and believing in the project's worth, then the consultant likely has the kind of communication skills the project requires.

Related to their ability to "transmit" or communicate information to the client, and equally as important, is the consultant's ability to listen and hear what is said (or not said). To be successful, a consultant must have the capacity to stop talking long enough to listen. We all have been in the situation where we are in the presence of a so-called expert or know-it-all and have typically come away from that experience feeling a sense of unpleasantness. However, compare that feeling to the one we experience with a close friend, advisor, or confidant who truly takes the time to understand what we are experiencing and feeling and then provides insight or counsel. Or compare an encounter with someone who is focused on demonstrating how much they know and is using us as the vessel to do so, versus an encounter with someone who has our interests at heart and is not seeking to remind us of how far we have to go before we are at his or her level, but rather how much we can do to reach to our goals.

Trait #5: Hunter vs. Gatherer

The consultant's world is not too far removed from an earlier time in our collective history when the choice was either to eat or be eaten, and many of the waking moments spent on this earth were focused on that very choice. A consultant *must* be comfortable with the *constant* need to do battle (metaphorically) to ensure that there is sufficient food (revenue) to satisfy either him- or herself or the tribe (the consultant's family). Many competent and experienced people who qualify as "expert" in their chosen fields will not succeed as consultants because they lack the ability or tolerance to put him- or herself on the line time after time and prove that they are still capable of "putting bread on the table."

One of my friends, Luci Sheehan of Wendell Park Associates, has spent her career working as a consultant, hiring consultants as a senior-level executive for both large and small concerns, and working with/developing consultants who have at various times reported to her. She is fond of comparing the successful consultants to "hunters": those people who are eager to venture away from the campsite and chase down the next meal through their own cunning, guile, strength, or other measures. She compares them to other perfectly successful people in most settings, i.e., "gatherers": those people who are able to recognize opportunities when presented to them and nurture them to their full benefit. Luci's insight is that while it helps to have both skills resident within a consulting practice, it is the hunter who is celebrated, and with good reason. The gatherer waits for circumstances to arise where he or she can take advantage of a superior intellect or skill, and the hunter creates situations and is more in control of his or her destiny. A consultant too reliant on the next harvest without benefit of an existing one is one who cannot sustain the farm waiting for the change in seasons.

While this list of consultant traits is not all-inclusive, it does illustrate to a potential client that consultants (1) are likely to be self-reliant people who work well autonomously (hunters rarely travel in groups), (2) are able to communicate up and down the organization in a way that is compelling and infused with confidence and enthusiasm, and (3) are equally comfortable dealing with issues that are content-based on their area of expertise, as well as business matters that trend to the more pragmatic (expense report follow up, scheduling, etc.). A client that looks *solely* for a consultant with skill in one area (expertise) might be frustrated when the consultant is unable to work within the business processes of that client company, such as the consultant who proclaims, "Time sheet? I don't fill out a time sheet. That is why I don't work full time for a company!" As a client, choose a consultant who is competent to handle the rigors of the assignment and comfortable with adhering to client standards of protocol.

Experience

The experiences that most consultants have in common are:

- Competency
- Comprehensiveness
- Control

Consultants must have experience that demonstrates their competency to themselves and others. If the consultant has had little to no relevant exposure or experience in the area in which they are specializing, it would be a rather hard sell to try to convince a client who might be skeptical to begin with about one's background or expertise.

Of course, what is considered relevant experience and what is deemed to be competent can be disputed between those assessing situations, but there is no denying that the consultant must pass the competency test in at least his or her own eyes before attempting to sell a client. The challenge is for the client to ascertain if the level of competence is suitable and appropriate for the situation currently being discussed.

How to judge competence is addressed later on in this book, but with no two situations being exactly alike from client to client, it is incumbent on the client to recognize if prior experiences can be deemed to be examples of competence or not (and if it is relevant competence).

Related to that point is how comprehensive the consultant's exposure or experience is in relation to the current client's situation. The client must determine if the consultant has seen enough similar situations to recognize when different approaches or options might be suitable. Unlike the proverbial "if I have a hammer, then every problem is a nail" solution approach, a client must know if the consultant is suitably prepared to identify and address opportunities that are related to, but not exactly the same as "the one of these that I did last year for another company" type of situations. Unlike going to a local tavern or even barber shop and asking for "the usual" and knowing that you will be satisfied with the result, consulting problems are rarely as easily met as that.

A good consultant must also be thinking in terms of how the recommended solution will impact related functions or initiatives. For instance, in my consulting practice, I often train salespeople in effectively managing their trade funds budgets (used as an incentive to retailers to display products within stores to increase sales, or to lower prices temporarily to induce consumers to try a new product in the hopes of getting them to switch and become loyal users of the new product). However, the company hiring me must be "on board" with the final result and not simply be training for the sake of training. If the client does not reward salespeople for efficient spending of trade funds, but rather still sends the salespeople who sell the most product—regardless of how far off they are on their budgets—on the all-expenses-paid trip to some exotic locale, then I would be remiss if I did not point out that salespeople's behaviors will *not* change for the long term. It will take *only* one year under that system before the sales force recognizes that, while they know *how* to manage their trade funds and managing budgets, there is no real incentive to do so, and in fact, there is a strong *dis*incentive to do so (they lose their ability to compete with the salespeople who do not manage trade spending and therefore are at a competitive advantage for incentive trips).

The last experience that clients expect consultants to have is control. Does the consultant have experience making the decisions that impacted the results being shared as their competency or comprehensiveness? Is the consultant someone who was "on the team" but was not making the decisions that guided the process, or is the consultant someone who was responsible for "making it happen"? This is not to say that *only* the person in charge can be a consultant, nor is it suggesting that the person in charge would be a better choice for consulting assignments. All it suggests is that from an experience base, the client has a right to demand that the consultant must have had significant responsibility in ensuring the success of previous assignments, or must demonstrate an ability to do that on the current assignment. While we all can fantasize about the person in the mailroom who is given a shot at running a company and succeeds, the Walter Mitty fantasy rarely leads to clients being willing to spend any sum of money on an unproven talent.

Purpose in Life

The cynical among us might think that the purpose of a consultant's effort is to hobble the client so sufficiently, but not totally, as to become dependent on that consultant for longer periods of time than the initial assignment. While that might be unduly harsh and caustic, it is not without at least a germ of truth or kernel of insight. Consultants learn early on that they should approach a client with the third project in mind (sell the third project first). What that means is that rather than just addressing the initial assignment and upon the conclusion of the project collecting the fee and moving on to the next client, the consultant should look to expand the project to multiple phases and inquire about other needs that can be met or solutions that can be provided by the consultant. On the face of it, this is not a nefarious undertaking, nor is it necessarily ill-intended. A good consultant should be aware of the intersection of other factors on the success of a proposed project and, as a smart advocate for the client, should be advising about other opportunities to strengthen the client's position vis-à-vis other initiatives. And many consulting sources (books, audiotapes, lectures, etc.) recommend that in forging a relationship with a new client, it is shortsighted to *only* think of the preliminary assignment and not focus on the longer-range implications of any actions within that first assignment on the potential long-term relationship. This approach makes sense and is logical from many different perspectives; however, if taken to heart by some consultants without being completely understood as to the motivation behind it, it leads to consultants who might intentionally look to embellish project scopes or create anxiety about the "holes" in a proposed approach to a situation. Now, to be sure, I am not casting aspersions at *all* consultants, nor am I suggesting that this is a common occurrence—but it is something that a new client unfamiliar with consultants must be vigilantly testing to ensure that only the right project scope is being proposed. But safest of all for a client is to deal *only* with ethical and proven consultants known for their advocacy *for* clients and not *to* clients on their own behalf.

Interestingly, one of the first experiences I had with this perspective of selling the third job first was when I was an ambitious, but very green, 27-year-old manager of training for Symbol Technologies, Inc., and I was tasked with overseeing the work of a consultant who had been hired by a more senior-level manager within the company. This old veteran consultant took me under her wing and answered many of my questions about the business end from the consultant's side of the equation. After a night of "tipping a few back," the consultant looked at me with bloodshot eyes and slurred, "David, consulting is a hurt and rescue mission." Then, content to have just shared the inner meaning of life with me, she went back to her libation. When I appeared perplexed (even in her state of intoxication, she was able to discern that I was confused), she followed with, "If the client is not already bleeding on the floor when I get there, then I cut them and allow it to flow for awhile ... only once they are feeling desperate do I then offer them a solution and it usually costs more than they would otherwise have paid ... but until there is panic, I can't be hired." I thanked her for her sagely wisdom, excused myself, and filed that away as something to think about later on when I was in a better position to ponder it. I am still pondering it and still thinking if it is truly accurate or not.

So What Does a Consultant Do?

A consultant can work across any function or division within a company and can be responsible for a whole range of projects from the most mundane to the most innovative and secretly created (lest the competition become aware of some radical new product or production methodology, or come to know that they themselves are the target of what falls under "market intelligence" or corporate espionage tasks where a company does what it can to better understand its competition and their approaches, plans, and initiatives). However, regardless of the scope of the consulting assignment or the internal employee directing the consultant's efforts, there are broad classifications of activities that consultants engage in with clients. Few consultants will reside *solely* in one of these classifications and, in fact, *most* projects will require a hybrid of the following approaches. However, for purposes of explanation, I shall treat these as if they are separate and discrete approaches.

Consultants can provide **advice** by sharing their insights, recommendations, and suggestions for the future of a company (or a division, a corporate function, etc.). The consultant in this instance would be hired mostly for their "visionary" strength and wisdom and would be expected to provide the avuncular guidance that we all associate with a "gray-haired eminence who has successfully been through the wars" and can now impart their experiences to the next generation of leaders and managers. The advice provided might be fairly general in focus—that is, it could be applied as easily to one company as to another, but is highly sought after and valued because it represents a radical departure or split from conventional thinking. An example of this would be the work of W. Edwards Deming and his focus on Total Quality Management (TQM). His popularizing the notions of efficiencies and removing waste from production and other processes within our companies led to a rash of consultants and legions of advice providers who would impart the Principles of Quality and reinforce their importance to the client. But these consultants were not hired to change the organizational structure, nor the processes, but rather were brought into the client's company to share their insight into the future wave of business.

Consultants who work off of this model tend to be very passionate about their approaches or theories and vary little from it. They believe wholeheartedly in it, and while they might permit slight variations and permutations on it to fit a specific industry or company, they would not veer too far off of their original view of "what it takes to succeed" or "how the best companies address the 'x' issue."

Consultants are also hired to provide **analysis**. Unlike the consultant who strictly provides advice, the analysis-providing consultant does not enter the relationship with the client with a ready-made answer in search of a home, but rather walks into the client with a series of questions that will then be answered through the course of the assignment. These consultants pride themselves on assuming a certain amount of "professional ignorance"—although they are fully versed in the needs of the business and are fluent in the language, challenges, and successes, they do not assume that they know the answers to the perplexing questions a company might have. Rather, they focus on their understanding of how best to answer the questions through their skills at acquiring and synthesizing information. The sheer number-crunching, multi-variate analysis that often goes into market research or strategic planning requires skills in asking the right questions, in the right ways, at the right times, to the right people, and then projecting a series of "what-if" scenarios to determine the appropriateness of certain actions.

I previously worked for a consulting division of a large market research firm that provided analysis to the consumer packaged goods industry on factors such as at what price points to sell an existing item without unintentionally going lower than absolutely necessary to attract consumers, what consumer demographic to target for a new product introduction, where a product would sell best in the "shelf-set" as shoppers walked the aisles of their local grocers, etc. There used to be *huge* turf wars between the consulting division that I was a part of and the teams of people assigned to supporting specific clients in fulfilling their data needs. The core of the conflict came down to whether we as a consulting division provided any additional benefit beyond what the client-servicing personnel were already offering. As you might imagine, lines were drawn, positions were hardened, and few people on either side of the debate moved measurably in one way or another off of their original position.

It was our contention as the consultants that without the context to position the analysis (rows and columns of numbers and pretty-colored graphs and charts) into meaningful action, there was no true consultation being offered, and the analysis provided was really just data that *someone* (likely within the client organization) was going to have to review and make informed decisions about what actions to take as a result of their assessment of the data. Now, to be sure, there were many among the client service teams within the market research firm who were providing this kind of analysis to their clients on their behalf. And whether they are referred to as consultants, salespeople, or client service providers is less important than the fact that they were offering *consultation* to their clients based on the information collected. The employees who were merely dropping off the latest series of reports or "run" of data and not providing insights were doing their clients a disservice. Data and information delivery is *not* the same thing as analysis. Analysis in this instance involved the complexities of understanding trends (Are consumers increasing or decreasing their use of a particular product over time?), likely responses of competitors (Will SC Johnson stand by while Procter & Gamble introduces a new product, or will they introduce one of their own?), and impact on organizational efficiencies (Can the same salesperson sell this product on their current sales call to the retailer, or do we need a new "go-to-market" approach to handle this product's sales?). This information is rarely available in one source and requires melding disparate resources, weighting criteria during decision-making synthesis of seemingly unrelated facts, projections, and the odd mixture of quantitative processes driven by computational expertise with a fair amount of qualitative and creative flair for uncovering insights that most would miss.

Consultants also are at times called upon to **develop products** on behalf of their client companies in the broadest sense of the word. Is a salesperson who sells a software application that is customized to the specific needs of the client not performing in a role that is consultative? Where the boundaries are for selling a product that is to be incorporated into the processes and inner workings of a company and where the work of consulting begins and ends are hard to discern, and it might be pointless to even try.

In recent times, the word *salesperson* has unfairly conjured up images of a slick-talking, joke-telling, commission-based, say-anything-to-get-the-sale type of person. To combat that, some sales forces have changed the names of their jobs to remove the stigma attached to that career and are now calling themselves account executives, product consultants, or other less objectionable names. Regardless of what the position is referred to, the role of many salespeople blurs into that of consultant as soon as the "sale" is contingent upon the client having to integrate the product purchased into their business. For instance, the local office supply store salesperson is not "consulting" with the buyer when selling paper clips, but the salesperson who aids in the design of a filing system in addition to selling the filing cabinets, electronic media, or other filing and memory devices might be considered a consultant.

A consultant (or salesperson) who provides an improved methodology through the use of a piece of technology or a tool, or accomplishes a desired business outcome through the application of a product they sell to a client (or customer) is consulting to that company in a meaningful way. While we might not think of the salesperson as being "in the same league" with Peter Drucker, Michael Hammer, Tom Peters, or other leading consultant gurus, the fact remains that the integration of the product into the client's business processes (as opposed to a product that is tangential to the processes of the business or is used for resale by the company) is a consultative endeavor.

The next approach that some consultants use is the **sale of a service** on behalf of the client organization. That service might be theoretical as in the case of a consultant illuminating the most recent thinking on employee motivation as it relates to non-sales positions, or a client might desire assistance in the creation of a marketing plan, a software application that is proprietary to that particular client, or a brochure to be used by the sales force to sell a new item to customers. In each of these cases, and many more, it is not uncommon for a consultant to have either contributed to the creation of the service as part of a larger team or to have even been given the lion's share of the responsibility for design, development, and delivery of that service to the client. Consultants who work in this realm will often spend a good part of their time actually on the client's premises and work with identified subject-matter experts within the company. To a remotely located employee who does not go into the office and work face-to-face with corporate-headquarter personnel often, upon meeting the consultant there might be confusion as to whether this consultant is really an internal employee. Consultants who work to create services on behalf of clients and are co-located at the client's work site are often seen as being indistinguishable from internal employees by others. The consultant works to maintain that sense of being "part of the team" and often interacts across many different departments.

Important to note is that clients *rarely* buy a consultant based on the above work provided. In most cases, you as a client will be more interested in purchasing a *result* (e.g., less absenteeism, shorter sales cycles, reduced time between billing and payment). How it is done is of less consequence to you as a client, than the fact that it is actually accomplished. Therefore, a consultant might choose to use a hybrid approach as necessitated by the project's parameters to accomplish the end result desired. It is not essential that one perspective or approach be used over others. What is essential though is that the client be comfortable with the methodologies employed to achieve the result. The focus is on the successful result or outcome. Few will remember or care about the details in getting there, but many will recall the effectiveness of the solution.

What Consultants *Don't* Do

Clients might choose to use consultants for many different roles within a company and might choose to have the consultant provide their contribution or conduct their business according to any of the above approaches. However, clients should be mindful of certain caveats (and consultants would be wise to conform to the following simple constraints as well) that go beyond the very fundamentals or basics of business ethics that we all should subscribe to (recent corporate events of mismanagement and reporting of earnings not withstanding).

Consultants are *not* responsible for managing the client's business and results. Some clients might be swayed by promises of "I can get you 'x' more points of margin by providing you with this newfangled approach to forecasting," or "I can cut the time to produce your widget in half," or other claims. As attractive as these pitches might be to a client in need, they are beyond the scope of the consultant's ability and should be immediately discounted and seen for what they are: "sales fluff" based on the consultant's misunderstanding of their role and capabilities. *No consultant* should be tasked with providing results, nor should a consultant be volunteering to assume that responsibility. Until that consultant actually sits in the chair of the executive within the company and is formally tasked with that job, there are too many variables that can impact the successful attainment of expected results.

If the country hits a recession, if a competitor introduces a new product, if the company does not fund an initiative fully, or a whole host of other unexpected confounds occur between the time of the original plan's creation and the expected result, is the consultant accountable for things beyond his or her control? Too many clients too willingly abdicate their responsibility for results to outsiders in the hopes that they can spread the blame for it when the solution does not produce the desired results, and too many consultants are overzealous (or perhaps ignorant) in assuming the responsibility for factors that are outside their ability to control or influence. Although an internal employee is equally at the mercy of unexpected results as the consultant would be, the internal manager is in a better position to impact the other variables that might support a particular initiative (staffing, resources, permissions, etc.).

One of my mentors in thinking about consulting and the role of consultants to client companies is Mike Bosworth, formerly of Xerox, then Solution Selling (his own company that he founded on the principles he learned while working at Xerox), and most recently CustomerCentric Systems. Mike is fond of sharing with his clients that consultants (or salespeople) should never approach the assignment as if they are a replacement (temporarily or otherwise) for the executive who hired them (or for anyone else in the company). The consultant is to consult to the executive, even lead the executive through the decision-making process, provide counsel and advice, etc., but is *not* to assume the role of the executive and make decisions *for* that executive. Ultimately, the client will be responsible for that decision's impact on the organization and, as such, must not be usurped by a consultant willing to take the mantle of leadership from that executive for the duration of the project.

There is room for a consultant to sell their services and potential outcomes to the client on the basis of what others (referenced preferably) accomplished through the consultant's assistance, or in sharing with the client what *they* might be able to accomplish through the use of a consultant-provided solution. A smart client will quickly associate the consultant with that result and want to replicate it if it is an appropriate initiative to pursue, so there is little chance of the client missing the point that the solution is linked to the consultant's ability. From a sales perspective, if you tell Quaker how Kellogg's already achieved success, you will get their interest more readily than if you approach them and attempt to sell them based on unsubstantiated claims or promises of accepting responsibility for results. The client community often knows that a consultant cannot deliver on promises outside their sphere of influence anyway, and as it relates to consultants assuming responsibility for results that are internally derived, a smart client will not be swayed (and should be critical of the veracity of that consultant's other commitments).

This will have important implications later on in the process of managing consultants, evaluating consultants, and in separating from the consultant at the conclusion of the project or in the event that the project is not progressing as expected. However, for now, it is important to recognize that the consultant's role is to provide input of one kind or another (see prior section), but not to replace the executive or become an internal employee subject to the pressures of running the business. This last point is a controversial one and will be addressed when compensating consultants is discussed later on in the book.

What Consultants *Shouldn't* Do

A consultant should properly address each client from the perspective of what that client's needs are and what solutions would be *most* appropriate for that client given a whole host of intervening variables (problem identification, objective of the solution, corporate culture, timing of the solution, budget, resources, internal subject-matter experts dedicated to the project, etc.). Clients need to be wary of consultants offering to "do for them what was done for someone else," without demonstrating a complete understanding of that client's unique composition. Consultants who are promoting "canned responses or solutions" to business problems real or imagined are truly not consultants, but are entertainers who recite the equivalent of a business script and do little more than distract the client while fleecing their coffers.

Therefore, I advocate that clients think of their consultants the way they think of their physicians and hold them to a similar standard as it relates to diagnosis and prescription. In my consulting practice, I often ask prospects and clients what they would do if they awoke with a scratchy throat. Most tell me they would ignore it the first day or so and hope it would resolve itself or at least not interfere with their daily tasks. Then I ask what would happen if by day two or three the scratchy throat had not improved. By then, most people would attempt to self medicate: drink tea, consume chicken soup, or take whatever over-the-counter medicines they typically use for sore throat symptoms. If, by the fifth day there was no relief, most of the people I ask this of would seek attention from their health care provider. I then present the following situation: "If you are brought into the examining room area, but not examined by the health care provider at all, and then you are told to take three tablets and eliminate certain foods from your diet for the duration of the sickness, how likely is it that you would take the prescription as directed?" Invariably, there are those who would feel the interaction was not appropriate or complete. Although it is *likely* (though not definite) that the health care provider has probably seen a number of cases with similar symptoms, was correct in their diagnosis, and chose the appropriate prescription to combat the illness, the absence of an examination and the attempt by the health care provider to better understand the situation (When did it start? Is it more painful after or before eating? Does it hurt here or there? etc.) leaves many of us feeling the suggested solution is inappropriate or at least cannot be trusted.

Consulting offerings should be treated the same way. A consultant who has not gone through an equivalent examination of the client's business needs and demonstrated an understanding of the client's situation to the client's satisfaction is doomed to failure. Prescribing a solution without having diagnosed to the client's satisfaction is an invitation for disaster for both client and consultant.

Checklist for Defining a Consultant

When considering hiring a consultant, be sure to ascertain the following and designate Yes or No by placing a check mark in the column describing the consultants you are evaluating.

	Yes	No
Traits of the Consultant		
Belief in the value of the service provided		
Confident in own ability to complete the project as structured		
Has a perspective of the "business" and not solely the "problem"		
Excellent communicator		
Has the aggressiveness necessary to be a "hunter" on your behalf to get things done		
Demonstrated Experience of a Consultant		
Competent		
Comprehensive		
Control		
Approaches Taken/To be Taken		
Advice		
Analysis		
Production/integration of service or product (custom)		

Why Use a Consultant?

Key Learning Points:

- Reasons to use a consultant
- Implications of using a consultant
- Whether to use a consultant or internal resources
- Political implications of using a consultant

---

executive ability: the art of taking all the credit for the hard work done by others

The reasons and rationales for using consultants are vast. Some clients minimize their use of consultants and prefer to use them only in the most desperate or trying of circumstances when there is seemingly no other option available to them. Other clients see positive strategic implications in using consultants: These clients never consider consultants as the absolute last choice available, but rather recommend and expect their organizations to use them where feasible. And of course, there are those in the middle—the great majority of clients that fall in between those two polarities of opinion and action—that use consultants upon occasion and view their use as appropriate in certain circumstances or situations.

From my own experience as both a client who used consultants and now as a consultant to industry executives, the least productive time to use a consultant, or at least the time to have the minimum expectations of the consultant's contribution, might seem counter-intuitive to some readers. If consultants are called in to "bail out" an executive when essentially "Rome is burning" and time is of the essence, they are rarely able to bring the full measure of their experience and knowledge to the client. Clients might think these times would be ideal for a consultant: "We only need the consultant in these times of crisis. We are able to manage the situations that arise on a daily basis just fine. It is the extreme, out-of-the-ordinary situations that require someone with more background, resources, and exposure to methodologies." What happens more times than not in these situations is that the consultant is constrained by the following:

- Previous commitments made by internal employees ("I pledged to my boss that I would get that software integration done in the second quarter and it *has* to happen or I will lose face!")
- Oversights ("I did not realize that Marketing would care if we saved a few cents on our production costs by lessening the packaging expenses and reducing the amount of color used on the label.")
- Mistakes ("How was I supposed to know that employees cared about being able to access their corporate e-mail from the road— I don't travel on business!")
- Errors ("It never occurred to me to ask our Information Technology Group if they had any interest in being represented on the team determining our sales order entry system. I figured it was a 'sales' issue.")

Being constrained by situations such as those listed above forces the consultant to make decisions that are hasty and might sacrifice quality for meeting a deadline.

A sign that appears in my local dry cleaner's store sums up the dilemma quite nicely, "Your inability to plan is not my call to action—it will be ready in five days!" Unfortunately, few people use that dry cleaner because of the unwillingness to rush certain jobs. Within the consulting profession, the overwhelming majority of consultants who have been in business more than three years can likely share their own stories of having to accept projects that were required to be completed in times far too compressed and at a sacrifice to the potential benefit of the project had it been better paced and scheduled. Some consultants willingly accept rush jobs and simply charge higher fees for the inconvenience of being forced to cut corners, rush, provide less than their best work, and just meet a deadline.

Rather than have my own in-house production facility that reproduces manuals, workshop materials, presentations, or findings reports, I use a local printer that I have established a relationship with over the years. This printer is fond of telling new customers unfamiliar with how service providers operate the following: "You, as a customer can choose two out of three options. But I will choose the third. You can have it cheap and fast, but I will be unable to do a very high quality job. You can have it fast and high quality, but it won't be cheap. You can choose to have it high quality and cheap, but it won't be done fast. The choice is yours. I know that as a customer, I might want all three, but practically speaking, I will be unable to accomplish all three. One of them will have to be compromised."

I see the same things occurring with the kinds of consulting projects mentioned above. Clients find themselves behind the "8 ball" and then seek relief from their own shortcomings, but expect the consultant to magically create answers without having completed the due diligence that so often is required to provide true "value-added" benefit. Of course, this also leads to clients and consultants accepting "square pegs for round holes" in an effort to meet a deadline and explains why there is such a proliferation of standard, one-size-fits-all solutions. These solutions are seemingly easy to implement, though any client can affirm after trying to do so that what seemed possible on paper becomes a whole lot harder in actuality *because* it is not a solution geared for that company specifically. In addition, these solutions appear to resolve the issue for the moment; however, both client and consultant are engaged in an activity that approaches an ethical gray area when they use "cookie cutter" solutions. Hiring the consultant to do what the client *should* know will be ineffective and the consultant had *better* know is not designed to succeed is really not in the organization's best interests and leads to blaming behaviors, lawsuits, and hard feelings when down the road the results are not what were expected and the finger-pointing begins and culpability must be assigned.

Reasons to Use Consultants

There are times—other than just the extreme situation described above—when it makes sense to use a consultant. While some situations are "better" than others (to be subjectively determined by each client), they all do occur with some regularity according to the clients and consultants I have come in contact with:

1. Some clients seek outside expertise that cannot be found or is undeveloped internally. When staffing (and especially in our current economy when so many companies are looking to become as efficiently staffed as possible to reduce fixed costs and overhead), many companies will not see the economic value in hiring and paying full-time salaries and benefits to "specialists" who are called upon only rarely (if ever) as an "insurance policy" in case the need arises. While most smaller and mid-sized companies will need the recurring skills of a bookkeeper and will hire one, a full-time accountant on staff might be judged to be beyond the needs of that company. That same company might occasionally contract with and use an attorney for trademarking or copyrighting products and advertising campaigns, but will not have that person on staff as corporate counsel to handle future lawsuits or other legal issues that are as of yet, unidentifiable. In these examples, it makes good business sense to "pay as you go" for the services of an expert that a company does not require on an ongoing basis. From a client's perspective, even if the fees charged for the consultant are more than it would cost on a "per-project basis" had the company hired someone with that background to join their staff, the economics of *not* having to pay for the services when the

person's skills are not utilized more than make up for the incremental costs incurred for the project fee.

My own consulting career evolved in many ways from the sporadic needs of companies to use someone with my background, but few needing to have someone with my experience work for them full-time as an employee. I have a background academically and experientially in instructional design (the study of how to best create opportunities for learning in its most simplest explanation, though I confess that even after I explain it to many people, they still look glazed over as to what it is I actually "do"). While many companies have trainers in-house and either use commercially available workshop materials or create their own "home-grown" content, these trainers very often are ill-equipped to address the custom training development needs that crop up within companies from time to time. The backgrounds of these trainers might vary, but often the people in these roles are former "job incumbents"—they previously held the job they are training others to do. The logic behind using a job incumbent is that they know what it takes to do the job, so they can train another to do what they did and be successful. Furthermore, they will be good trainers because they will have credibility with the participants—after all, they did the job side by side with many of the people they are training and can share "lessons learned." Or some trainers might be more aligned with the employee development side of training, and while they are not content gurus or subject-matter experts, they are people who are interested in ensuring that training is a productive exercise and work hard to structure training sessions that are beneficial.

On a more cynical note, I once worked with a new director of training who called me in to assess the strengths of his department, but shared with me that upon meeting his newly inherited team, he felt that he had just been bequeathed a "turkey farm." His opinion was that he had been given the people who had outlived their usefulness in other departments, but were still valued for their stories of the "good old days." Others in his newly acquired group were nice enough folk and did not "deserve" to be let go, but just were not quite capable of positive impact in their previous roles, so they found a home in Training. Still he found others who were neither nice, respected, or competent, but were retained because they were the people that "time forgot," or at least the people who had always been there and somehow it seemed wrong to get rid of them now.

There are occasions in the work I am called upon to do where a particular client will decide that a project is beyond the capabilities of the available resources to complete it and will hire me as an "expert" in the design, development, and delivery of training either to create a workshop from "scratch" or to cobble together from multiple sources a workshop that incorporates the best thinking of many. My business partner, Jeff Clow, refers to this cobbling as my "Betsy Ross projects" because I am weaving together fabric from many corners of the organization to create "the flag." Once the project is complete, the needs for my services conclude (until the next time a similar project taxes the abilities of the current staff and I am re-engaged for that project). If no projects requiring my expertise are planned or implemented, the internal resources available are sufficiently skilled to address the day-to-day issues required, and the client doesn't have to pay me to sit around just in case something should appear that is beyond the group's competency.

2. Another use of consultants that many progressive clients employ is to contract with highly skilled people to consult with them or their staffs on an issue that is currently beyond the capabilities of the internal employees. But rather than just "farming it out" to the consultant, the executive uses the consultant as a mentor or instructor for the internal staff. The consultant does not "just provide the output or finished product," but also is required to instruct the internal employees on the process, approaches, methods, tools used, etc., so that the internal employees can then accomplish the tasks on their own the next time it is required. Of course, this is a more effective strategy when:

   • The internal staff is sufficiently skilled, is knowledgeable, and has the ability to perform the task once trained.
   • The task is a repetitive one that will be required again in the future (and preferably the near future before the newly trained

skills erode from lack of use). If the task is unlike future tasks, then the benefit to being trained to address the current task might not transfer as easily to the next task.

• The consultant is a competent instructor and willingly shares approaches, methods, etc.

Some consultants would balk at the idea of doing this under the belief that they would be grooming their competition. Even if the staff are not going to suddenly seek consulting assignments, the fear is that the staff that would have once sought the consultant to perform the tasks will now do them without the consultant, and therefore, the consultant will lose a revenue opportunity in the future. Other consultants would view this assignment as an opportunity to deliver additional value to the client and to become differentiated from other consultants who are essentially "vendors" to the buyer—they sell their time or product/service, but don't necessarily become viewed as strategic partners and have the kind of access and opportunities that strategic partners typically share. The consultant who chooses to accept this assignment is banking on being perceived as someone who is trusted and a part of the team and someone who will be willing to potentially lose a little now to, again, potentially gain more down the road.

Some clients have recognized the value of using experts in particular niches or content areas, even those that are relied upon heavily or frequently and are essential to the functioning of that corporate department, based on the ability to spread the existing full-time staff across more projects and initiatives. In this way, fewer internal people on the company's payroll are needed because the project work is being done by others who are contracted with to handle the unique requirements of each project as it arises. In this scenario, the internal person does not need to be overly specialized in any one discipline or field of endeavor, but rather must be aware of the overarching goals, take a comprehensive view of how multiple projects—each assigned out to different suppliers in some situations—are to be brought together to form the whole, and remain focused on how best to maximize the efforts of the hired consultant so that the contribution made by that consultant is greater than it would have been had the work been brought in-house.

I first experienced this approach to using consultants when I worked as a manager of training at Symbol Technologies, Inc. I had (mistakenly) thought I had been hired for my background in training, my ability to create written materials that would assist the salespeople on their sales calls, and my understanding of how best to structure the transfer of knowledge and skills to those who can most use it to build the business. While those things likely did contribute to my getting the job, I was to learn that the job itself was less focused on those aspects and more focused on making sure that the vendors selected to do that work were performing due diligence and following the practices correctly in the development of the work they performed on our behalf. Being somewhat exasperated at seeing work that I considered myself to be qualified to complete going to outside vendors, I scheduled a meeting with my boss's boss to discuss this, at the suggestion of my immediate supervisor, so I was not "going above" him. The possibility that I might not have been as ready for the assignments as I perceived I was never entered my mind. I even fancifully thought that I could do even better than what was being done by the outsider since I "knew" what we needed, could talk to those who were going to use the materials, and could edit/revise/modify as needed much more quickly. So on trembling feet, but with the righteous indignation that I had at what I perceived to be a slight at my abilities and a waste of corporate resources to be hiring others to do work that we—that is, I—could do in-house, I was ushered into the office of the more-senior executive to discuss my concerns.

After listening to me lay out my case as to why I could do better, why it would be in everyone's best interests for me to do the work, how I was going to improve on the work that was being done, etc., he fixed his pocket square (he always wore a complementary pocket square to his tie, but never the same pattern), fixed a stare at me, and then as if I was the most simple person he had come across, he began to explain to me (as I wilted in front of him) that whether or not I could do better work than the consultant was of little concern to him (I detected that he did not believe that I could do better, but was throwing me a bit of a "bone" by not contesting it, but then quickly dismissing it). He further explained that he had 15 or so projects that were to get done by end of year and if he were to take me off of four of those projects to allow me the time to truly devote to getting the one project up to a level that was in keeping with my (overly?) high standards, that he would win the battle, but lose the war with his superiors. He told me he could not leverage the one (potentially) stellar project with those who evaluated his contribution to the organization to explain why the others were not done or were not done at least competently.

He was so adamant about this approach to business that he would use consultants even when his own staff was *not* taxed to the limit with work. He was of the opinion that consultants were not only to be used when the work was beyond the abilities of the internal staff, but also even when the staff *could* feasibly do the work in order to enable them to manage other assignments. While it was a blow to my ego to be thought of as an "administrator" more than a "doer" of projects, the reality was that he and his department did complete a lot more projects than they otherwise could have or would have had they taken the work in-house and done it without the benefit of consultants. As he dismissed me that day to go back to juggling four projects "well," but none "superbly," he introduced me to two different concepts that I have now run across a time or two as a consultant:

- **Vendor manager over content expert** when selecting internal staff. It is better to have a person working internally who is more comfortable directing and guiding the experts in their chosen fields than it is to have a specialist on board. If the expert is an internal resource, then the company is limited in what they can expect of that person. Most companies cannot afford to have "designated hitters" who do not play out in the field when the game involves being able to hit, run, catch, and field. Waiting around for the once in a great while when the designated hitter gets up to bat and hoping that the person can always produce huge results is a fool's game. Better to have people who are conversant in multiple disciplines, choose vendors who are comfortable working with that staff, and reward the consultant for jobs well done by providing as much business as is feasible and allowing them to learn and know the organization as much as possible to break down the constant "educating of the consultant" practices that would otherwise be necessary.

• **Progressive performance over postponed performance.** This executive believed that it is better to show partial progress and build on it successively if necessary than it is to delay and wait to try to build the perfect project. He would rather have made inroads and shown some forward movement than to take the time to try to make the project's output perfect. In his mind, the perfect project would never happen. There would *always* be something to tinker with or some improvement that could be made. Rather than strive to get it to that level, he was in favor of doing a high quality job today and admitting to himself that he will have to readdress it in the future to pick up the things that will change over time or that were not accounted for in the original project formation. Better to demonstrate that there was improvement over what "was" than to promise what "will be" the result, and have no results to show in the meantime.

I can't claim that I enjoyed working for him or in his department at all times, as his approach and mine did not always mesh. However, I have come to appreciate that his approach to consulting and use of internal resources did make some sense in certain circumstances (such as a fast-growing entrepreneurial company, which Symbol Technologies, Inc., was at the time). As I often think of business in terms of sports analogies, I came to realize that what he was suggesting is akin to using his department members to "play a zone defense" against projects (each person had a series of projects they were to cover, but none of them were to take precedence over the others on an ongoing basis, and as soon as a project was to the point of moving on, attention was to be paid the remaining projects) and not structure the assignments within the department on a "man-to-man" basis (in other words, don't assign a project to a person and expect that person to be with that project and that project alone through every developmental step to the exclusion of every other project).

3. Some clients choose to use consultants to address issues that they view as being politically important and feel that a consultant offers them better opportunity to accomplish their goal according to political criteria as much as more "objective" evaluation variables. It is important to remember that as a client considering bringing a consultant into your company to meet the needs of the project, the affiliation with the project and the consultant can be wielded both positively and negatively by the primary contact person to the consultant within the company (as well as others within the company) and needs to be managed with an eye toward political ramifications in addition to the merits of the project's output and the consultant's contribution.

Savvy clients (and I use the term *savvy* as neutrally as possible) will recognize that the relationship established with an outsider to address internal issues provides wide leeway to permit tangential concerns beyond the project's supposed "intent" to factor into the success or failure of the project.

It is not unheard of for topics that are controversial or have the chance to reflect poorly on the company's decision makers or management to be "farmed out" to a consultant so that when the "inevitable" results (recommendations, suggested changes, analysis, etc.) of a project are received by management and the organization at large, there can be a distancing of the message and the messenger from internal resources. Rather than have management have to "take the heat" for a decision that is unpopular or impacts the organization negatively (layoffs, reduction in benefit plans, or other "difficult to communicate" actions), management can place the "blame" at the feet of the consultant for coming to the conclusion of the harsh reality confronting the organization. No longer is it, "We as a management team have decided to...." It now becomes, "After contracting with the consultant to investigate ways to avoid having to make this difficult decision, we were advised that there is no alternative but to...." Management can take the role of "advocate" for the people impacted: "We tried to find a way around this, and we had your best interests at heart when we began this process, but the consultant told us that in spite of our best intentions, in order for us to remain competitive, we were going to have to walk this path. As difficult as it is to have to implement this, we are counting on you all to work with us, as we have worked for you, to see to it that we succeed and revisit this situation after we have corrected all that the consultant identified." The hope is that management will be seen as working for the common good of all and that the consultant will shoulder (often anonymously since most within the company will not have met the consultant or had interaction with him or her) the burden for being the "bearer of bad news." Consultants often do not mind being put in this light as they recognize that they are being hired for the purpose of reducing the heat on management, and as long as they perform their jobs capably and admirably and don't provide inaccurate or inappropriate counsel, they have performed the job to the best of their abilities and can take solace in the knowledge that they "made the tough suggestion" because it was the most appropriate one to make given the parameters of the project and needs of the client.

In the course of the ebbs and flows of business cycles, there will be times when senior management will want/need to show "good faith" or validate their approaches with those taken by "best-in-class practitioners" or approved of by recognized experts. Sometimes, stockholders will need convincing that management is truly performing their role to the benefit of the organization; other times, internal employees might appreciate the added comfort of having independent advisors offer their approbation of management's actions; and still other times, customers and/or suppliers might request that management confirm their approaches with recognized experts in particular disciplines before they offer their support for management's actions.

In each of these situations, management is choosing to use a consultant for their objectivity and recognized *gravitas* as an expert to support management's actions, or at least lend weight and strength to the claims of management for a specific action. Management might feel (correctly so) that there are obstacles or hindrances to accomplishing their stated objectives that are borne of cynicism or remembrances of past actions that did not turn out well. Rather than try to bully their approach past the various constituency groups referred to in the previous paragraph and risk additional resistance and negative outcomes as a result of that approach, management will choose to seek a consultant to confirm management's approach, assuage hard feelings, or mollify the impact to those adversely affected.

In this way, the consultant offers endorsement of the decisions that management would otherwise have had held up to scrutiny by those non-believers, and management is able to reduce the friction or feet-dragging that typically follows a difficult decision that involves changes within the organization. No longer is it management (the people you view as perhaps not knowing best, or question if they had done the appropriate research before selecting a course of action) making the decision in a "vacuum," but it is now management in concert with a leading authority on these matters—someone who is professionally recognized for addressing issues *just like this*—reaching the same conclusions.

Again, I caution clients, do not apply the "shackles" around the wrists of the consultant, limiting him or her to "find and report back to us only what we tell you to." In addition, the process must be completed in an objective way without undue influence (and offering to pay the fee only if the final outcome is aligned with management's suggestion qualifies as undue influence). When these two practices are avoided, the consultant can provide the equivalent of "expert testimony" to those who need the extra reassurance, even if it is the management team themselves who just want to be sure that they are not missing anything before they take steps toward a particular action.

Similarly, management teams might choose to ask a recognized authority (such as the latest popular business book author or lecturer) to approve of the actions that management has taken or plans to take. By so doing, management is able to subtly say to those who would question their actions: "We brought in *the* expert in this field and she/he endorsed our approach, and therefore before you come looking for our heads or question our approaches, be sure you know what you are talking about."

Management personnel employed by a client also might not be sure themselves as to what steps to take to correct or address a business problem being experienced by the organization and choose to use a consultant to accomplish two things simultaneously. The first is obviously the hope that the consultant will uncover a recommended

approach to address the business issue that to this point has con-
founded management (Why isn't the product selling? What is the hold
up in production? How can we get accounts to pay more quickly? etc.).
The other intention that management might have is to simply buy time.
In the intervening time between contracting with a consultant and
the day of reckoning in the future when results will be expected, it is
the hope that business cycles will change and the problem will correct itself, divine intervention will occur, other issues will supersede
this one and it will no longer be on the minds of people, or any other
outcome. What management is hoping to do in this situation is "call
a timeout" and stop the clock from ticking temporarily: "We are looking into various options to address the situation and have retained the
services of XYZ Consulting Group to assist us in exploring the various
possibilities, so in the meantime get back to work, keep doing what you
have been doing, and let us figure this out on our own." By electing to
have the consultant participate in the process, the client is stalling the
naysayers from having their turn at criticizing management. Logically,
management has the upper-hand to now say that they are quite aware
of the issue and are addressing it by bringing in the consultant. It is a
positive step in most situations as it demonstrates that management
is proactively going after the "best and brightest minds" to ensure a
beneficial outcome. Taking their job very seriously, management has
secured the services of a renowned authority to ensure that the process
includes not only the thoughts of management, but the ideas and practices of the consultant (who one would be led to believe is current and
aware on the leading edge practices being implemented at the most
successful companies that have addressed this issue to date).

Some consultants might not like assignments under these terms and
refuse them on the basis that they are being asked to participate in a
manipulative endeavor that is really not focused on resolving the issue
as its primary purpose, but rather is a ruse designed to bolster management's standing with their constituencies. As a client, it is hoped that
this would not be the purpose or approach taken by the reader, but it is
fair to raise it and explain it as a way that consultants are used by some
companies. While the ethics of it are somewhat "gray" and involve
shades and degrees as opposed to absolutes, consultants are occasionally used (hopefully not with their full knowledge and involvement) to

create the appearance of activity by management, with little expectation of implementation of suggestions or recommendations.

In the cases where management is unclear of what steps to take and has a bias toward taking action to correct the issues that prevent success, there are times when calling in a consultant is a politically advantageous thing to do. Aside from the benefit of having the experience and knowledge of the consultant applied to the project and the expectation of a solution that is as good or better than the one that management would have crafted on its own, the public relations value of aligning with a consultant can reflect positively on the client company.

Members of management are proactive enough to know that when confronted with an issue of such and such magnitude, they went right for the expert (Consultant "A") and were up front enough about it to tell us (constituents) that they were earnestly looking to resolve the issue as well as they could. A client that secures or a manager within the company who chooses to hire the consultant with the experience in this realm or discipline surely is someone who takes their job seriously and is allotted a certain hands-off time period to sort it all out. You can't be too critical of a person or company that recognizes the significance of the effort and went and acquired the insights of the person or people who know the most about this topic.

Rather than go with an "also-ran" type of consultant, a client can leverage the fact that they hired the best and share in the "reflected glory" of being with the best. For a while in the information technology field, any manager who chose IBM machines could not be criticized too strenuously. While there might have possibly been better solutions available to that manager to choose from, surely no one at the time could think poorly of a person who chose to go with the leader and most stable option (even if the cost was higher than a competitor, there was value in being an IBM customer). Not unlike today, if management is concerned about demonstrating their commitment to an initiative that involves strategic planning, Boston Consulting Group is likely to be one of the firms mentioned, and if the project is international in scope, McKinsey & Company will probably receive a high frequency of references.

For the reader who has gotten to this point and wants to object to the seeming communication issues embedded in the above, or takes issue with the "us vs. them" scenarios being painted, I remind you that as much as physicians speak of taking preventative steps to maintain health, most of us rely on the physician *after* the symptoms of an illness are present. While there are *whole* hosts of ways that consultants can and should be used to address "healthy" situations, it is imperative that we not lose sight of the fact that more times than not, the consultant is being called upon precisely *because* there is an issue that requires addressing.

Before we leave the topic of politics and consultants, there is a political double-edged sword that does impact the success of consulting projects from time to time: how closely aligned the primary client contact is with the consultant and the relative status of that person. As a client, the intention should be on the project, on its own merits, and not on some gain to be achieved by association. However, we must recognize that in the competitive world, there are limited opportunities for advancement and chances to "shine" in the eyes of others, and the possibility to position oneself for promotions is at times few and far between. Being responsible for bringing in a consultant is one of those times that can impact the future career path of an employee.

On the positive side, success in choosing a consultant and having a project deliver on or exceed expectations is a "feather in the cap" of the executive wise enough to have seen the need and taken steps to address it. Credit for the success of the project, even if it is a wide-scale project that incorporated many people's efforts, will be assigned to and shared among those who are most closely affiliated with the project's execution. Being associated with a successful project and being recognized as the person who managed it to completion is often a quick road to ascension within corporate ranks. A quick look back in history points out the backgrounds of U.S. presidents after time of war: the successful generals who served during times of war often were viewed as being (at least in part) responsible for the victory and therefore were able to maximize the positive feelings among voters associating their skill in war to their skill in leading the country across other disciplines (economics, policy making, etc.). Surely, everyone loves being connected to a winner, and by being seen as responsible for the victory (in this case, having the foresight to bring in the consultant who eventually allowed the business to succeed and managing the project well), many a career has been enhanced.

On the downside, being too closely aligned with a consultant can also raise doubts, fears, or mistrust among others within the company. If an internal person is viewed by peers as being "the flunky" for the consultant, that person's credibility will suffer because the connection with that consultant is not being viewed positively. Also, if a project requires the cooperation of multiple people and those people do not "like" the primary client contact assigned to work with the consultant, those people can choose to diminish the project's effectiveness by not offering full cooperation. If the consultant is seen as just the "mouthpiece" of the executive and is not truly offering objective counsel, the output provided by the consultant will be discounted and the success of the project will be hampered (it will not be implemented or will not be given the same level of credence that it otherwise might have merited).

A personal anecdote that is related to the political implications of using consultants (this one has a negative ending, though it still illustrates the point) is when my business partner, Jeff Clow, and I did some work for a multi-national company that was headquartered in the Netherlands, but maintained a business division that was primarily located in the United States. We had been contracted by the vice president of sales to deliver a custom-developed training workshop that incorporated skills in negotiating, financial management, and presentation development. In working with our local contact in the United States for this international project, we had asked what sensitivities people would have to being videotaped practicing a "role-play situation," given that it would occur in English and would require the attendees to participate in the role play in what might not be their native language. Our concern was not to embarrass anyone who did not feel comfortable interacting with native English speakers in a role-play situation. Our contact considered it and decided that the workshop would be better received if we did not expect people to role play. We built a workshop that included the facilitators (Jeff, myself, and others) interacting and providing examples of the points (then asking the participants to critique our efforts that purposely included both positive and negative aspects), but at no time asked the participants to role play.

About halfway through the first afternoon of the workshop, a senior executive from the European headquarters asked our client contact, one or two attendees who were *not* part of the development discussions, Jeff, and me to meet with him at the next break. Thinking we were going to be complimented on how cleverly we had met the objectives and demonstrated the salient skills without having to ask the participants to role play, we were blind-sided when this senior person asked why we were not videotaping people and analyzing their strengths and weaknesses. He then turned on our client contact and stated, "This is not what we agreed to, and I know you did not author-ize the training to *not* include the most important aspects, did you?" Our client contact (remember, this is a vice-president–level person) realizing the political implications of standing up to the more senior-level person at this moment and assuming responsibility for providing us with incorrect or poor direction, wheeled on us and said, "We are expecting role plays and since you do not have them included in the workshop, I see no reason to continue with this. . . . It is a waste of time." I was stunned into silence at what I perceived to be a betrayal of the agreement, and especially when I had specifically asked about role plays in the development of the project. Jeff was not nearly as speech-less as I was and calmly explained that we delivered as contracted and were not at fault for not being prepared to address this new objective. Needless to say, the workshop did not go off as planned from that point forward, it ended early, the European executive was not pleased with the fee we charged (of course, after the fact, came the objection), and we never received additional opportunities to work with that cli-ent again (though if there is any justice in the world, that U.S.-based executive will have lost his job by now due to someone else deciding that he should be held accountable for arbitrary objectives that he was unaware he was to meet). Still, it is indicative of how quickly a client can align with a consultant when the perception is that it is beneficial to do so, or choose to distance oneself from the consultant and heap all that is wrong around him or her upon the consultant when that seems to be the more politically astute thing to do in some people's eyes.

Lastly, another political reason why some client contacts will use consultants is to gain exposure, and network or job hunt through the contacts of the consultant. If the consultant has a far enough reach into other organizations, it might be an expedient way to gain endorse-ments and be made privy to opportunities in other companies that otherwise would not be publicized. There are some clients that will ask a consultant who works with them to recommend someone to fill a position that will become available shortly, or ask if the consultant knows of someone with strength in a particular area. If an executive has worked with that consultant, there is a chance that the consultant might think highly enough of that executive to recommend him or her for the other company's position. While not done for this purpose alone, some client contacts will view the consultant as an excellent resource that will provide access to the "underground job market" that never hits the help wanted ads or reaches recruiters. The added benefit is that if a recognized expert (the consultant) endorses the potential candidate, it carries more weight than some other networking sources.

Working *for* the consulting organization can also provide a direct employment opportunity in some instances. The consultant might value the professionalism and effort of a particular client and might choose to offer that person a job to apply the skills currently used for the client for the consultant. A cautionary note though before the reader currently working in a full-time position thinks of this as a natural career path opportunity: Most consulting contracts that clients use with consultants include clauses that prohibit or at least attempt to reduce the "poaching" of talent between consulting organizations and clients. Not only is it often in violation of the contracts, it is also bad business practice in many instances to "mine for talent" at client sites (at minimum it is a good way to ensure there are no repeat requests for services from that client). Often forgotten in interactions between consultant and client is the fact that as much as we think we can hide what we do from each other, there are often "people who know people," and in many ways, we are all connected with only a few steps in between any two people or companies. A consultant who develops a reputation for stealing away talent will find more doors closing than opening from clients and prospects across many different companies. Invariably, the word gets out, and those consulting organizations are shunned, or the reverse, clients that develop the reputation for hiring away the consulting talent are often not provided with the best and brightest within the consulting organization's ranks (lest they be lost to the client). Although the dilemma is a bit different from the consulting organization's perspective than it is from the client's, having a "fan" of the consulting organization within the walls of the client is viewed as a positive by most consultants, and given that the client generates the revenue collected by the consultant, it is often something that is viewed as a "price of doing and maintaining business" to allow a percentage of consultants to willingly move over to the client side as a way of sustaining future business opportunities.

Identifying Consultant-Appropriate Assignments

Determining whether a consultant would be warranted to fulfill a project's obligation or is an appropriate option is subjective (as has been suggested before), and each set of circumstances and variables needs to be judged on their own merits. However, there are a few criteria that do tend to lean in favor of using consultants over internal resources (regardless of the company's tolerance for using consultants often or sparingly):

- Does the project *require* an internal person to complete it (can *only* someone internal handle the project)?
- Would having an internal person dedicated to the project prevent that person from handling other assignments and tasks that are of equal or higher value and importance to the organization (and can't be contracted out themselves)?
- Does the project involve expertise, skills, resources, or tools that are currently unavailable in the organization?
- Is the project able to be completed autonomously without tremendous interaction with others within the organization (can it be done off-site, or through phone/e-mail contact or infrequent face-to-face meetings)?
- Is there a benefit to having an "outsider" or "independent voice" conduct the assignment rather than a familiar internal resource?
- Are the results of the project likely to be controversial or cause negative feelings or outcomes? Does having a consultant as part of the process deflect criticism?
- Is the project in response to an internal issue that is better served by *not* having management or internal resources involved in it (investigation, analysis, reporting of findings, etc.)?

Assignment Duration

As a client, one of the most critical decisions that must be determined is the finite start date or time and the conclusion or stop point. Ideally, this will be spelled out between the consultant and the client, and will be addressed from another perspective when contracting issues are covered later in this book. But it is also important in choosing *why* to use a consultant. A consultant is appropriate to bring in for projects that have definable start and stop times (either pegged to a date or an event). It is reasonable to commence a project "from the time we receive FDA approval until the conclusion of BETA testing," just as it is more typically seen as "a start date of June 1 and a concluding date of December 1." Depending on the business needs and the amount of control one has over these factors, either might be sufficient. The essential point though is that a consulting project should have clearly defined points in it from beginning to ending. A consulting assignment that has no recognizable duration and continues on ad infinitum is not a consulting assignment at all—it is an employment contract!

In working with clients as a consultant and from my experience as a client and working with consultants, there is a feeling that occurs on both sides of the relationship that is understood, but not always spoken. From the client's perspective, the consultant is being "leased" for their expertise or ability to contribute and is not being bought or purchased (as one would with a full-time employee, making a more complete commitment to the person). At the end of the lease (duration of the consulting contract), the client can "turn it in" for a new model or choose to go about their business without the benefit of the services of that consultant or any other. From the consultant's perspective, many hardships and frustrations can be endured on client projects as long as the consultant reminds him- or herself that it is only temporary and that at the conclusion of the project, the consultant need not ever work with that client again. The sense of there being a "finite" start and stop to the relationship should either party be dissatisfied with it allows both parties to retain a psychological safety that actually serves to keep them together and productive more times than not. Because they each can walk away from the other in a relatively short period and they feel they control that, there is infrequent need to do so. The reminders they each tell themselves that the project has a defined beginning and ending allow them to focus less on what distracts or disturbs them and more on getting on with the work and seeing to it that the project is completed.

Budgets

In my work with clients across different-sized companies, varying sophistications, and diverse approaches to business, I have encountered a phenomenon that some client contacts have used to their advantage. Not all clients budget or apportion the cost of using a consultant in the same way. Some client departmental budgets treat the acquisition of consulting resources under budget lines that are tracked as part of personnel costs, and others include the cost under something closer to capital expenditures (equipment, office supplies, etc.). Still others will split the cost of a consulting project across multiple budget lines (allowing the travel and entertainment budget to absorb the cost to fly or put the consultant up in a hotel as necessary, pay for a product or service contracted for out of a project line item budget, and pay for the consultant's time out of a discretionary budget or a personnel expenses budget).

What this has allowed certain clients to do is make more efficient use of their departmental budgets to maximize the value and breadth and depth of the projects and initiatives they can handle. Projects that would otherwise be beyond their ability to fund had they used internal resources are now within their capacity to complete and fund. The reasoning is you are already paying for an internal employee, so you can't charge their time and compensate them against allotted dollars for non-internal employee expenses. Without suggesting any underhanded or nefarious slight of hand in using budgeted dollars, smart managers have understood that it makes sense to use consultants in certain situations from an economic standpoint, resource allocation, and project management basis.

Appropriateness for a Consultant

Before going off and trying to reinterpret corporate budgets and stating your case for how you can find ways to include consultants in your current roster of projects due for the year, be sensible about whether a project is appropriate for the consultant. I have found it helpful to ask my clients that are wrestling with this decision to ask themselves these four questions:

1. Is this project critical to the organization?
2. Will the output or result of the project warrant the expense of doing the project?
3. Is the project best served by using a consultant or can a better result be achieved through internal resources?
4. Does the consultant need to do the project now, or is there no jeopardy or risk to having it done sometime in the future?

In determining why to use a consultant, the last point to be made is to be sure that both the consultant and the client are clearly aligned as to what the reason or purpose is of having the project completed by the consultant. There needs to be uniformity in the expectation (as obvious as it might seem to the reader, it is not always known) or the rationale for the project. Is the consultant expected to provide perspective and a worldly sense that is currently unavailable to the organization hiring him or her? Is the purpose of the consultant's efforts to produce something that is tangible (beyond a findings report or summary document) and is to meet certain criteria (software testing, etc.)? Will the consultant be expected to execute a workshop or produce an advertisement strategy? Is the consultant working for one or more executives (a committee) and therefore answering to multiple people? In making the determination *why* to hire a consultant, it is essential that the above be answered and shared, or there could be issues down the road in managing the project that were entirely preventable had each party known up front the answers to those questions.

Refer to Figure A to help classify your thinking on why hiring a consultant would be an appropriate action to take. Figure B raises issues that might preclude hiring a consultant, and Figure C addresses the politics involved in hiring a consultant.

Figure A: Why Use a Consultant?

Organizational Culture	Immediacy/ Urgency	Culpability	Need for Customized Solution	What is Needed	Duration
Organization is in favor of and has used consultants before	Need a solution *now*	Not looking to dodge responsibility, being proactive	• Just needs an "industry"-accepted solution • Requires custom solution	• Outside expertise • Mentorship • Political implications	Clear start and completion times for project
Organization does not use consultants, does not perceive value of using outsiders	Not a rush, can wait for internal resources to complete	Trying to "save face" for internal mistakes	Requires custom solution	Inside resources *must* complete	Poorly defined start and stop time of project parameters

Figure B: When *not* to Use a Consultant

Check "Yes" or "No" The more "Yes" checks, the less appropriate it is to hire a consultant.	Yes	No
1. Are you hoping to "push" the responsibility on to the consultant for the results?		
2. Are you hoping to use the consultant's connections to "save" you from a bad employment situation and possibly place you elsewhere?		
3. Are you unwilling to admit that the consultant's objectivity might be viewed positively by constituents?		
4. Will having a consultant involved "block" you from receiving the accolades or benefits of a successful project completion?		
5. Are you/your company distrustful of the experience and relevance of outside resources?		
6. Do you doubt the value of using consultants to "mentor" or provide additional perspectives to your team?		
7. Are you distrustful that consultants have any basis for being expert in *your* company and *your* situation?		
8. Is this project not especially time-sensitive? Is it able to be delayed until other internal resources can address the issue?		
9. Does the project necessitate having a resource available to others within the organization at all times?		
10. Is the project without definable "start" and "conclusion" times such that you are unsure when the project would officially end?		

Figure C: Political Reasons for Using Consultants

Check Yes or No to decide if a consultant would be benefi-cial to your situation. If no check marks are in the "Yes" column, you likely do not need a consultant.	Yes	No
1. Need the "independent or recognized expert" to support management's approach to a situation/confirm appropriateness of a previously made decision or response		
2. Want the analytic vision of an outsider to ensure that management is including the best options in a decision they have yet to make		
3. Provide time to management (or others) to form a plan to address a mission-critical issue by acquiring better insight than they otherwise would have access to		
4. Want to be aligned with a progressive leader (author or other industry thinker) to take a competitive advantage over others in the market		
5. Need the ability to diffuse controversy over a decision by relying on "the best thinkers" addressing the issue on our behalf		

Selecting a Consultant

Key Learning Points:

- Determining the factors or considerations to use in selecting a consultant
- Identifying what your expectations are of the consultant's background/skill/experience
- What to avoid in choosing consulting assistance
- The value of reference checking
- How to determine the scope and criteria for successful consulting projects

There is something that is much more scarce, something finer far, something rarer than ability. It is the ability to recognize ability.

—Elbert Hubbard

When the work to be completed within a particular company (or department/function/team within a company) is either beyond the capabilities of the personnel or human resources available to do it or the work is better suited for an outside resource to complete, the pursuit for a consultant begins. But how to best do that and take the steps to ensure success (or at least minimize risk) is not well understood. Just like the Battle of Waterloo was alleged to have been won on the playing fields of Eton, choosing a consultant requires preparation and forethought.

What to Do

The selection of a consultant will be greatly influenced by factors that the potential consultants for the assignment will not even be able to provide. Before any consultant provides you with their fees, their references, their experiences with other projects, or other "proof" that they are the appropriate selection for a project, you will have to do the following:

1. Identify desired outcome
2. Define the project
3. Determine the project requirements
4. Assess the "value" of the project
5. Decide on the necessity for a "cultural fit"

1. **Identify the desired outcome.** The absolute first step to be taken is to identify what the end result of the project will be. Being able to complete the statement, "At the end of this project, I will know it was successful when I see … /because I no longer hear our customers saying … /based on market position, sales figures, or some other metric/etc." will help you determine a successful end result. Having a vision of the project's outcome directly influences how the project will be completed, what criteria will be used to measure its impact, and obviously, what consultant will be selected to complete the project on your behalf.

This step is what drives the subsequent steps, so its importance cannot be overstated. If you are seeking to improve morale as an outcome, your project will differ greatly than if you are looking to restructure your product pricing to keep it in line with current market conditions.

Very much related to this topic is the determination of how the project's success will be evaluated and measured. Deciding this forces focus on exactly what is important. If I want to improve employee job satisfaction, do I measure absenteeism (and therefore develop a project that addresses that specifically), or do I look to build a new incentive system (a much different project)? Even more fundamental, some would ask the question, "Why look to change employee satisfaction at all?" Employee satisfaction is typically a symptom of a larger issue that would need to be addressed before employee satisfaction could be changed.

2. **Define the project.** The way the project is defined will immediately remove most consultants from consideration and will provide some with a competitive advantage over others. The catalyst for the decision to hire a consultant might be an immediate drop in performance or productivity, the anticipated introduction of a process or software application to support the work done by employees, or the loss of market share to a competitor. However, within each of these general or global business concerns lies multiple project definition possibilities. Is the issue to be resolved one of selecting better-skilled employees (in which case the consultant you hire should have a background in skill assessment, recruitment, or sourcing)? Or is the project one related to improving the skills of existing employees to get them to perform better (and therefore, the consultant sought should have experience in training design and development, adult learning, and related skills)? Or is the assignment to be focused on building or creating better products/ services (which places the project in a context of being best handled by a consultant with exposure to marketing, manufacturing processes, or other areas that are entirely different than the prior two examples)?

3. **Determine the project requirements.** One of the words that gets tossed around a lot when consultants and prospective clients talk with (or about) one another is the word *scope*. Scope refers to the parameters or boundaries of the project. Many consultants are often accused by clients (prospective or ongoing) of looking to expand the scope of a project prior to contracting in an effort to secure higher fees (as the scope or parameters of the project increase, the cost to the client increases, and the consultant is provided with a larger contract). Conversely, many consultants often counter-accuse clients of attempting to contract for a

small project and then use "scope creep" to ask the consultant to perform additional duties: "As long as you are doing that, would you mind also doing ... " (of course, at that point, the client is not thinking of paying for the additional work, merely viewing it as a favor to be done since the consultant is already performing related functions or would not have to invest any *real* effort to do the newly requested task). On the other hand, some unscrupulous consultants will use that technique to their advantage by bidding for a small project and then looking to expand it into a much larger project midway through as they "uncover" additional needs and stress the urgency of addressing those needs to ensure that the desired outcome occurs as anticipated.*

Obviously, if a project warrants modification due to unforeseen circumstances, then a decision needs to be made as to whether the original project scope still makes sense to maintain or, if the project has so completely been changed, is no longer appropriate to pursue under the original agreement. In the course of my own consulting career, I have been asked to add or subtract portions of an original contracted-for-project "deliverable" due to information that had not been available when the project was first agreed upon or to changes in strategy or corporate direction that rendered certain portions of a project obsolete or at least less critical to future success of the client company. In those situations, a mutual decision is made between the client and me as to whether it makes sense to simply replace consulting service "x" with consulting service "y." For example, a client might ask, "Instead of interviewing our managers about their subordinates' performance, would you mind interviewing our customers about our salespeople's skills?" In those instances where it does not change the overall project complexity or does not change the size of the project and level of commitment required to complete it, I might agree to "zig" instead of "zag" as part of the project. In other instances, I have told clients that it is not an equitable swap to have me develop a two-day workshop on negotiating strategies in place of facilitating a planned strategy discussion with senior management (there are implications beyond the

---

*For an excellent and easy-to-read example of this in action, I recommend *Soldier of Fortune 500: A Management Survival Guide for the Consulting Wars* by Steve Romaine, Prometheus Books, Amherst, NY, 2002.

obvious here that we will return to when we discuss pricing services, but as a "teaser": Not all consultants sell the time they devote to a project as the barometer of the value they provide). Clients can then decide either to stop a project mid-stream because it does not make sense to continue or make changes to the existing agreement, allowing the project to move ahead with modifications. While these situations can and do crop up and are at times unavoidable, it is highly recommended that the project be clearly defined up front prior to a consultant being selected and that consultant commencing any work.

More common than these situations is the confusion that occurs between client and consultant as to which party will provide what services/support/participation in the work of the project. As a client, are you prepared to offer or provide the following?

- Office space within your site
- Equipment including hardware and software, and ID numbers to permit physical entrance to corporate locations or even past electronic security or firewalls for projects requiring that access
- Access to decision makers (and not just an internal telephone directory of all employees, but actual introductions and meetings)
- Subject-matter experts assigned to the project (and if they are assigned, will they be dedicated exclusively to the project, or will this assignment be above and beyond their current jobs and be fit into their workday as availability permits?)
- A project sponsor (someone who will take ultimate responsibility for the project's progress and is usually highly placed enough to remove roadblocks or obstacles in the way of the project's completion)
- Copies of prior work done related to the project and owned by the company (from internal employees or other vendors who have provided work contractually, but is owned by the client firm)

Rather than establish roles in the client-consultant agreement, it is far more often the case that client and consultant will make assumptions about the responsibilities each will have in completing the project. If these responsibilities are not confirmed and included in their agreed-upon project-requirement understanding, the opportunity for conflict and a poorly managed project increase exponentially.

4. **Assess the value of the project.** One of the most critical steps in selecting a consultant will be making the determination of just how important/critical/vital this project is to the company or the people affected by its completion. Earlier we mentioned that among the reasons for pursuing outsider assistance is either the desire to off-load work that could have been done by internal resources, but was strategically better completed by a consultant, or as a developmental exercise for less-experienced employees to learn from someone with greater experience in a particular discipline or skill. As an example, few projects have greater value placed on them than the work that was done around the "Y2K" transition. Not many businesses were willing to view those projects as venues for employee learning and certainly were not going to permit project deadline extensions, as failure to meet a very real deadline in that situation could have led to dramatic negative impacts.

Depending on the urgency, skill required to complete the assignment, tolerance for errors, and ability to "learn as you go" on a project, the value associated with the project's successful completion will fluctuate. Obviously, if a project is less "mission critical" to a company (in other words, it does not impact the future viability or success of a company), a manager would be more likely to use the project as an opportunity to have a less-experienced employee and consultant complete the assignment. If a company's success hinges on the completion of the project, the consultant's experience, background, and credibility become much more salient features in the decision of which one to select than if they are a "friend" or come across as a "nice person and fun to be around."

Looking at it from the consultant's perspective, projects are more likely to carry much larger fees when the value to the client company is understood to be huge. They are also less likely to be delegated to more junior members of the consulting firm, as the visibility on these projects is usually such that it is too critical (for both the client and the consultant) to take a chance on the project not being handled by the best-matched resources. Consultants, being aware of how projects that are more core to the client's business success are viewed and treated internally, will often bill for those projects on a "value basis"; the fee is in part reflective of how urgently the client needs to have it done right and done quickly, and their willingness to pay for that assurance.

5. **Decide on the necessity for a cultural fit.** When selecting a consultant, the "cultural fit" between the consultant and the client company is one of the most often used criteria. In essence, the client considers, "Is the consultant 'one of us'?" That is, is he or she formerly from the same industry or background? Does he or she look and act the way management does? Was he or she educated in the same schools? Now, to be sure, there are times when that might actually work in reverse— when the consultant desired is expected to be *different* in experience and perspective than management to prevent a "sameness" of approach when a dramatically different approach is required.

A consultant who subscribes to one methodology or approach that is in conflict with the preferred business strategy and tactics of a client will usually not work well with the internal employees since their paradigms are so vastly different. It is only natural that corporate employees (this really applies to people in general, but we are focused on corporate employees and its impact on them) would prefer to work with people who are more similar to them than not. The level of comfort one has with someone they identify with and share common viewpoints with is obviously higher than it would be with someone who was perceived as being dramatically different.

Within cultural fit discussions, there is room for diversity of opinions, though it is perhaps clichéd to point to Information Technology departments and notice that the casual approach to dress (hair, clothing, and even hygiene in some instances) is celebrated as a sign of brilliance and creativity of thought coalescing in a person who can't be bothered with the mundane tasks of "looking presentable." Yet, the Sales and Marketing departments with their emphasis on customer contact and appearance would not be nearly as tolerant about tattoos, dangling earrings, and feet in beach sandals bereft of socks.

Before leaving the topic of cultural fit, it is necessary to also point out that an executive must explain to the employees within the department/function/whole company the following:

- Why the consultant is needed. Clarify and answer questions that are asked by employees who might not be as familiar or aware of your thinking and might misinterpret the rationale behind the necessity of a consultant as an assessment of their future.
- What the project and consultant will be expected to deliver (that is, the results or outcomes).
- What *you*, as the executive, are prepared to do to see to it that the project is completed correctly and delivers the results you seek.
- What commitment you are asking of other employees to assist or contribute to the success of the project (that is, time, resources, access, etc.).
- The ultimate decision-making process. Will this decision allow employees to have a "say" in making the determination or will they be merely advisory? Or perhaps it is a decision that will be made by more senior managers, and employees will not be consulted on the selection, but will be expected to support it and work well with the consultant.

Vertical or Horizontal Expertise

Consultants are generally classified according to two variables:

1. Vertical expertise
2. Horizontal expertise

A consultant who is vertically focused is expert within an industry and is comfortable crossing multiple functions for project work. An example would be a consultant who is very adept in utilities and is adroit at handling marketing, engineering, and administrative function projects for utilities, but would be uncomfortable working in a media or market research company because those are foreign industries to the consultant. On the other hand, a consultant who is vertically focused within consumer-packaged goods manufacturers might feel competent to address brand marketing, sales, and distribution consulting opportunities, but would be ill-at-ease working with the heavily government-regulated utility industries.

A horizontal expertise permits someone with a strong background in a particular functional area to address that function's needs regardless of the company's focus. When "Quality Improvement" efforts were the rage in the 1990s, many consultants felt quite comfortable consulting on the process and would work across many different industries, transitioning between and among them relatively fluidly. However, far fewer of those consultants would have dared attempted to consult on topics outside of their "Quality Improvement Process" work. For example, they would not venture into consulting on improving diversity among managers, or managing the exchange rate of foreign currency.

Still other consulting firms use a hybrid approach and have their feet somewhat in both camps. They are conversant in a small number of industries and, within that, are competent at a smattering of functional requirements. So, you might have a consulting firm that is very strong in technology companies that also has a presence in financial services and pharmaceuticals, plus is well staffed for assignments using skills in marketing (new item development, opening up new channels of distribution), operations (manufacturing, distribution, logistics), and human resources (staffing, development, organizational design). Firms that practice this approach can reasonably ensure that you will receive high-quality consultative support as long as your project falls within their matrix of industry and function.

Still other consultants do not define their contribution or even their work according to function or industry. They see their contribution as being more global or strategic in nature and, therefore, not constrained by these parameters.

Futurists (not people who look in crystal balls or recite incantations, but rather those who are more focused on current trends and their implications for the future) see themselves on a different level of contribution than other consultants. These people view their consulting work as being more awareness building and pondering of how different facts, disparate initiatives, and trends will coalesce to create a reality that might not be intuitive to the unobservant. Perhaps the best and most recent examples of this kind of consultant are John Naisbitt of *Megatrends* fame and Tom Peters of a more recent vintage. By taking information not normally collected and compared side by side to answer questions about the future, these (and others like them) have opened the eyes of executives to switches in the marketplace before, or at least as, they happen.

What Not to Do

Before the consultant is even hired and begins to work for you, a great deal of thought goes into laying the groundwork and foundation for a successful consulting relationship. In addition, you must ensure that the wrong things are not inadvertently done to hamper ultimate success. Ensuring that there is alignment between motives, expectations, and requirements of the consultant and the client company can prevent many negative outcomes from ever arising.

Among the most common areas where clients and consultants incur conflict are when:

1. Managers and executives wish to use consultants for personal agenda reasons that are not in the best interests of the company, nor the successful resolution of a stated business opportunity. Related to this phenomenon is the use of consultants as a vendetta against others within the company. If the culture of the company is such that the "project sponsor" or person with budgetary authority over the consultant is viewed as wielding both formal and informal power, the political use of a consultant can fend off challenges to ideas, intimidate others with differing opinions, or hijack strategic initiatives and prevent them from adversely impacting individuals, departments, or functions.

2. Clients expect an off-the-shelf solution to a highly custom problem. Consultants, doing due diligence and working to provide the most appropriate solution to a business issue, might identify that a problem cannot be resolved with a simple "patch" or "shrink-wrapped" solution that is a syndicated or generic answer that applies equally well across many different companies. In some instances, the project requires a unique response that might "borrow" from other work that has been completed, but is not sufficient in itself to meet the business need of the client. Clients and

consultants are strongly advised to reach agreement on the match between specific business opportunities and existing solutions to prevent this from occurring. Don't prematurely determine that a pre-existing solution matches a problem.

On the other hand, consultants benefit from the perception that a project is highly custom and requires much research or other unique and client-specific work when selling their services to a prospective client. This tends to drive the perceived value up ("This is a one-of-a-kind project, and no one else has ever done one like it") and therefore demands a higher cost associated with completing it in the way of consulting fees. Ethics aside as to whether the consultant is dealing truthfully with the client (and any consultant who sells a project as custom and then provides a one-size-fits-all solution deserves to have the wrath of both the client community and the consulting brethren fall down around that consultant's shoulders), the same decision needs to be reached: What solution matches the problem?

3. A consultant is hired for their expertise (be it a specific process they employ, specific insights they provide, experiences they can incorporate into a problem solution, etc.), and the client then requests that the consultant forego that which makes them unique and not deliver a recommendation within their niche area of expertise.

   a. A consultant who has been contracted with because of their creativity or innovative approach in problem resolution who is then required to use more conventional methodologies is not likely to provide the same level of insight and as high a quality solution as they might otherwise.

   b. A consultant who employs a rigorous statistically based process for uncovering market research insights and is then told upon being awarded the contract that all the client needs is their best guess is in all probability going to be uncomfortable with the project.

   c. A client that wants "an objective" view of the organization's management team, and then tries to dictate what the consultant's report should include is more than likely not going to allow the consultant to add the kind of value that the consultant was under the impression he or she was hired to provide.

This last one is the one that is particularly insidious for *both* clients and consultants. A client that steers a consultant to a conclusion (or a consultant who *allows* a client to either dictate or even informally guide the process to a pre-determined solution) is operating in bad faith. If the consultant is to be perceived as being objective and being an impartial observer from the outside, then there can be no steering of a solution (either subtly or overtly). Now, I am not naïve enough to suggest that in the interest of securing contracts, or furthering one's political or personal agendas, that this does not occur (in effect, "making a deal with the devil" to secure a result that is beneficial to one's own needs on both sides of the equation). However, it is something that besmirches the very process it is built upon—objective expert analysis and insight. Once the consultant is no longer trusted by the organization, other managers, subordinates, etc., the use of that consultant within the organization is called into serious jeopardy. The recommendations and observations are no longer viewed as independent and are not likely to be implemented with the same level of trust and "buy-in" as if that consultant was viewed as truly providing objective counsel.

Earlier, I shared an anecdote of how a U.S.-based executive at one of my firm's clients allowed another more-senior person to foul up a project based on that executive's perception of what *should* be done. That, in part, was an example of a person accustomed to "ordering" others to create a desired reality and did not distinguish between a consultant and a subordinate with a direct-reporting relationship. In this executive's mind, all that was needed was for him to stand up and mandate that what the organization needed was "x," and anyone who disagreed was to be ignored, bullied, or marginalized in their efforts to prevent his view from being implemented. At the time when he tried to do that with our project, my business partner, Jeff Clow, stood up to him and essentially told him, "You are the client and you can create whatever reality you wish for your company, but you will have to do it without our assistance." Our credibility and professionalism was not for sale that day and, I am pleased to say, had not been up for auction before or hasn't been since.

Where to Find Consultants

Once it has been decided that a consultant's assistance is warranted, the project has been (at least preliminarily) scoped out, and a general targeted outcome has been identified, the next step is to locate a consultant. It seems when one is *not* in the market for a particular service, a day can't go by without a solicitation offering to provide that service. However, since these solicitations are rarely filed or remembered for a time when you *will* need it, upon the decision to pursue a consultant, many executives are unsure of where to turn to source consultants.

The first places to look for consultants in a particular area of expertise are trade associations or industry groups. Nearly every industry has some association (and many have several) that provides member education, political representation, and opportunities for networking and idea exchanging between and among vendors to the industry and members. Whether at annual or more frequently held conferences or meetings, or at smaller regional get-together sessions, these associations provide access to both consultants with skills related to the industry or functional area of expertise you are seeking, and to others in the industry who have used consultants and can make recommendations based on their experience(s) with the consultant.

A list of trade associations can be found at:

http://www.marketingsource.com/associations/

Another frequently used approach to locating consultants within a particular industry or with a specific background is to attend trade shows or industry exhibitions where members and/or vendors will secure booth space and interact with each other as they attempt to sell products and/or services to one another. This approach is related to the one described above, but often these conclaves will also include presentations from industry thought leaders (consultants to the industry among them) or examples of successful initiatives (again, often with the assistance of a consultant who participates in the presentation) that might provide greater insights into what consultant(s) fit your need.

Many consultants publish books or articles for periodicals, and those materials are another excellent source for identifying potential consultants. A quick review of the bookshelves of your local library or bookstore or even a search of the electronic sites where you can review the contents of many books from the comfort of your computer will provide you with insights into the most current thinking on various issues, leading approaches, consultants who have a "point of difference" to apply to your situation, etc. This approach also provides at least a glimpse into how the consultant thinks and whether the consultant is a good fit for you, your company, and the project. Is the consultant very anecdotal in approach, or is the consultant more scientific and heavily quantitative in methodology? Does the book or article convey a tactical mindset, or is it more theoretical and analytic? You can determine what your needs are and if you feel confident the author/consultant would be someone who could accomplish what you need. These are just some of the more commonly assessed traits or characteristics that I have heard back from clients that have used my firm's services after reading some of what I have written for industry publications or books.

The best way by far to secure a consultant is through word-of-mouth. The experiences others have had with the consultant will carry more depth and "gravitas" than any projection one makes from either a presentation or a reading of an author's/consultant's thinking. If you know the consultant (prior experience with the consultant being best), or if you know the situation that the consultant succeeded within, you can make a much more informed decision on the likelihood of success in your unique situation than if you are relying on a consultant you are unfamiliar with or don't know the outcome of the consultant's efforts.

Second best is having someone you trust or perceive to be credible provide you with a recommendation of a consultant's abilities. If you don't have first-hand knowledge of the consultant, but you trust someone who has seen or had experience with the consultant and you feel is a good judge of talent, then this is another viable way to choose a consultant.

Working with a consultant is still dependent on the relationship aspect. For instance, if your view of the relationship is more sporadic contact and heavier reliance on autonomous and independent contributions to the project, can you work well with someone who demands frequent interaction and feedback? Ultimately, you will have to decide what factors or variables are most critical and if the consultants being considered are capable of meeting those requirements. Prior success is the best determinant of future success to be sure, but success in one circumstance does not ensure success in another. A bird successfully flying back home for the winter is a terrific feat, but I would not assume that success in navigating in the air would make that bird a good field guide for hikers!

On a related note, also be sure to establish whether the specific consultant assigned to your project is the person who sells the project concept to you. It is not at all unusual to have a senior-level person within a consulting firm sell a project under the (sometimes mistaken) belief that he or she will have an active participative role in the project (or at minimum, will oversee the work of less-experienced or junior members of the team). The reality is that in some instances, the more-senior member of the team who sold the project to you will make appearances only when the final presentation is due and will try to leverage that opportunity to sell additional add-on projects.

In these instances, the client company is charged "senior partner" rates for "junior and inexperienced productivity" and is used as a training ground for the lesser-skilled consultants to learn the job (all at your expense). Don't be swayed by vague promises of the gray-haired eminence promising to "have a hand in things" if the contract does not specifically spell out who will make up the team.

Earlier in my career when I worked for a different consulting firm, we had a reputation for doing very high-quality work in various consulting disciplines (strategy, research, and training). The founder of the firm was a "Renaissance man" in that he was capable (if not exactly comfortable) handling any of those tasks. We had other consultants/employees who were quite competent in handling one of those tasks, but not all of them. Upon occasion, we would have heavy project work in one arena and not another. While we did not often like to do it, we would "swap" out a resource from one division and assign them temporarily to another to cover a project that had a tight deadline. To the extent possible, we would try to "hide" that consultant with tasks that were supportive of the effort without unduly allowing their weakness to be exposed to the client. At no time, however, did that consulting firm ever offer a discount based on less-than-experienced consultants performing tasks for which they were ill trained and prepared for, and at no time was this "back filling" ever acknowledged or brought to a client's attention. The assumption that *every* consultant on the project was competent and experienced was a point of differentiation for the company in marketing materials, sales presentations, and contracts, and no client was to be given a reason to think differently.

Perhaps even more obvious an example of this is when a single consultant becomes closely aligned with a particular theory or approach to solving business issues, often through the publication of a book that captures the fancy of the business reader. Wanting to harness the power of that author's marketing "pull," the consulting firm will create a division or at the minimum will develop a strong selling story based on that author's work. The natural assumption of the unknowing client is that the "brains" of the approach will be part of the project team, but often, it is just not the case for many client projects. Without naming names, anyone who is familiar with the most recent spate of business "thought leaders" will also be familiar with the strong marketing campaigns behind those people aligning them with either the company that bears the name of that "thought leader" or a firm that is not at all shy about its association with that person. A natural conclusion is that you are "buying" that person for your project, but in actuality you rarely get that person; instead you get someone who might never have even met the person whose theory or practice is being sold.

References—Is There Value to Them?

Invariably, the question of whether to ask for references arises whenever clients talk amongst themselves about the best approaches to hiring consultants. From the "other side of the desk," here is what I would suggest:

Ask for references. However, understand the following:

1. It is rare that someone will provide a reference that will be anything except glowing.
2. Performance in situations similar to yours is what you seek, not overall performance, nor if the consultant is a nice person who is easy to get along with (unless you specifically seek a character assessment).

3. A reference should be current and should be based on "measurable" performance improvement (or some other metric that is beyond "easy to do business with").
4. Clients often will refuse to provide references or do not wish to be named in an effort either to protect their strategic intentions from the marketplace at large or because they view it as a competitive advantage that they do not wish to divulge. Knowing this, consultants will often rely on the statement, "We have experience in that area, but unfortunately, we are not at liberty to divulge with which client we completed that project as part of our confidentiality agreement with them."

It will be up to you to determine what is marketing "puffery" and what is a legitimate client relationship that is being protected as you would want your relationship protected as well.

Keep in mind that any information your consultant shares with you about other companies is likely representative of what that consultant is sharing about *you* with others. If a prospective consultant speaks ill of other companies/clients, provides details that are unasked for, and discusses things that you would rather were not shared with others if the consultant were talking about you and your company, you can consider that to be a red flag.

Certification

There is currently a large chasm within the consulting world as to the merits of being certified in consulting. The two camps line up on opposing sides of the argument and debate the issue essentially on two fronts:

1. Importance
2. Relevance

The first point is importance. Obviously, most of us would be more inclined to use a professional who has been licensed, has been certified, or has passed some objective exam prior to acquiring us as a client. Not too many of us would feel all that safe boarding a plane if the pilot had flown over a million miles, but only as a passenger! We would lack confidence if our physician had not passed medical school exams, or if accountants and attorneys had not passed their respective certifications allowing them to practice their disciplines. Yet, when it comes to business advice and consultation (legal and accounting aside), executives and managers rarely discern between those who that are certified by some governing body and those who are not.

The first question then is "Just how important *should* certification be to business executives?"(As we have already established and seen, it is not currently highly regarded.) In order to answer that question, we need to ask ourselves a couple of fundamental questions: "Is there a 'right way' and a 'wrong way' to perform consultation?" "Can consulting be 'graded' in terms of proper and appropriate versus improper and inappropriate?" After these are debated, the next issue is "Who will sit in judgment and decide what is 'proper' and what is not?" As if that was not contentious enough, the next question is "What should a consulting license consist of?" Is consultation the skill to be certified? Will it be partially determined on some subject-matter expertise in the area to be consulted upon?

Obviously, these are not easy questions to answer and at least in part explain why there is no unanimity among consultants and their clients on the importance of the licensure. Complicating matters is the way most consulting contracts are written that hold the advice-provider blameless for the actions management takes (even if based on recommendations from the consultant). Therefore, what real benefit is derived by the client for working with a licensed consultant?

The next issue is one of relevance. If a client is struggling with a thorny marketing problem, do they necessarily care if a consultant is a good consultant in any sense other than the one they are hiring him or her to perform? This analogy is similar to colleges and universities hiring excellent researchers and theoreticians as professors, and not those classically trained in education or teaching skills who might have an interest in the technical matter to be taught, but obviously would not be *nearly* as comprehensive in their understanding of the field of study as someone who has dedicated their life's work to that field.

While I offer no solutions in this matter, I do have a recommendation. It is a preference that each client and each consultant must weigh out and determine just how vital it is to the success of the project.

However, I believe that it can only benefit *both* client and consultant to establish some foundation on which to base distinctions and differences between service providers. The specific content of what the licensure must include still remains to be hammered out, but I perceive that there can be and are at least minimum expectations that can be established directly impacting the skill of consulting and being content neutral. In the absence of there being any guarantees of consultant competence and/or project success, it is worth the effort for a prospective client to determine what the key background, criteria, experience, and technical proficiency of the consultant might be, and then give consideration to the consultant's skills as a consultant.

Unique Contribution

Before rushing into a project with a consultant and authorizing that work be done on your behalf, it is appropriate to first determine if a project can be done with equal chance of success regardless of whether Consultant A or Consultant B completes the project. Said another way, is the project's success dependent on a particular consultant's participation, or is the project less specific-consultant dependent and more generic in skills requirement to be successfully completed?

It might be helpful to think of the differences in consultant skills and offerings in an analogous way to the different home improvement needs of home owners. Some people require the assistance of an architect to design and build a home from the ground up. Others do not need an architect, but are not prepared to take the tactical steps required to complete the vision they have for their homes. In this instance, a contractor or a specialist in a particular field (plumber, electrician, etc.) would typically be called upon. Lastly, a home owner might not need changes to the infrastructure of their home, but rather just cosmetic changes provided by an interior decorator.

Architect Analogy

If a project's success is predicated on using a proprietary process, software application, or other methodology that is trademarked by, copyrighted by, or in the sole possession of a particular consultant, then that consultant's participation in that component of the project (to the exclusion of other consultants at least as it relates to that one component) will need to be documented in the agreement between client and consultant.

Contractor Analogy

If a project requires a strong background in many of the industry's best-practices and experience with implementation or integration of disparate parts and processes, then a consultant with a varied portfolio of project work and exposure to many clients might be the most appropriate choice. In this instance, the "architect" consultant might be viewed as having a point of view that is too provincial, or might be considered to be too narrowly focused to see the implications of a broader picture. Of course, the specific needs of a project will dictate this, but the possibility remains that it might be more beneficial to work with a so-called "generalist" in this scenario and not assign the project to someone with a very strong detailed understanding of one facet of the project and who might seem to be myopic or unduly focused on only the part of the project that is nearest and dearest to that consultant's area of interest and expertise.

Decorator Analogy

In other projects, it might be most appropriate to work with a consultant who is known for, or has demonstrated a flair for, creativity and combining multiple approaches or practices to craft a new and unique way that is specific to the company and project needs. Rather than create a process from scratch, the project might only require someone with an eye toward recognizing patterns and complementary shapes and textures.

Martha Stewart Analogy

The last group of consultants in our home improvement analogy is akin to the role played by certain members of the media in helping the home owner make decisions on how to change their environment to accommodate the evolving living conditions and needs of the home dweller. The example I use is Martha Stewart to convey this approach to consulting. Martha focuses on using readily available resources (be it food, fabrics, gardening, etc.) and applies a wisdom or insight into maximizing the efficiency and effectiveness of that variable. She applies the suburban equivalent of home-spun wisdom that tribal elders have accumulated over time to assist the less skilled, less knowledgeable, or less aware members of the tribe to improve their surroundings. While many of us might not have thought of Martha Stewart in this light, she really does provide a consulting service that is not based on a proprietary process she has created. She does not often don safety goggles and attempt to use power tools to cut into walls or build attics, but she does provide expertise in home improvement projects on a smaller scale and one that meets a greater share of the audience's needs than the other approaches.

Other Factors to Consider

After the winnowing down of consultant candidates has occurred and only those meeting the technical requirements and the business competencies' needs have been identified, the awarding of the project must include consideration of other factors that are appropriate to the satisfactory completion of the project. These factors are to be assigned a weighting or strength in the final assessment based on the requirements of the project.

Speed. There are two components to the issue of speed. The first is whether the project requires an immediate solution. This means that the project must be completed within a defined time frame starting at or close to the current time. The second component to speed is from the time the project starts (in the future) until it is required to conclude, it must fit a proscribed time frame. Time frames vary because some projects need to start at once and will be completed within a defined period of time. Other projects might be part of a larger initiative, and as such, are scheduled to occur at some future point (sometimes undetermined), but once they begin, in order to remain on schedule across the larger and more complex initiative, this phase of the project must be concluded within a defined time slot. Obviously, from a planning standpoint for both the client and the consultant, it is imperative that the timing aspect of a project be clearly stated and understood. Especially when uniquely skilled consultants are to be assigned to the project, scheduling their availability within the parameters or confines of a project requires awareness of project "start" and "stop" times.

Cost. The cost issue is one that prospects and clients often get very focused on, and while important to use in selecting the most appropriate consultant for an assignment, it is not as well understood as it perhaps needs to be. The first issue with cost is to define what it is that is being acquired or purchased. Not all consulting services are valued the same by prospects and clients. If a project is more generic in skill requirement, then seeking a low-cost provider might be appropriate. However, there is something to be said for recognizing the difference between a specialist's skills and the expertise of one who is less practiced and proficient. In the context of medical procedures, very few of us would have a problem with a school teacher applying a bandage to a child's scraped knee, yet not many of us would line up to have that school teacher perform abdominal surgery on us (even if the teacher was a biology teacher). On the other hand, we don't pay the school teacher for his or her medical knowledge and are willing to accept and forgive the teacher if the bandage is applied in a way that causes pain from hairs being pulled off a child's leg. We are, however, willing to pay an orthopedist large sums of money if we suspect there is possible injury to a leg and wish to ensure that there are no broken bones. To be sure, the services provided are *vastly* different (bandage vs. diagnosis, treatment, therapies, etc.).

Most of us have had the experience of seeing a general medical practitioner for one reason or another only to be counseled to seek the opinion of an expert or a specialist. We typically appreciate receiving this advice and don't expect the general practitioner to "do the best he or she can" for the lower cost associated with that person's fees versus the specialist's fees. My business partner, Jeff Clow, has commented to clients with his tongue firmly placed in his cheek, "If you think consulting is expensive, try ignorance."

The cost is only half of the equation to be computed in deciding the appropriateness of a consultant's fee. The other half is the benefit or value derived from the services offered. If the same value or benefit can be received at the lower cost, then there might not be a need to pay more than that to another consultant charging a higher fee. However, before making that determination, a thorough understanding of what is truly being acquired for the fee requested is in order. As a prospective client, you might feel that the service being offered by the more costly consultant is more comprehensive than you need. On the other hand, after completing a side-by-side comparison of different consultants, you might decide that there is a difference in the values being offered and determine that you either perceive the value higher in one instance over the other, or go back to one or more consultants and ask for a reconfigured fee based on a similar project scope as identified by a competing consultant.

As mentioned elsewhere in this book, there are three variables that are being juggled on any one project: cost, speed, and quality. Ordinarily, any two can be acquired at the expense of the third. For example, a consultant can provide fast turnaround with high quality, but will charge a higher-than-ordinary fee, or a client can receive a high-quality and low-cost solution, but the project will be done in between other projects and on a time-available basis, therefore taking longer to complete.

Familiarity with the company. Another commonly used criterion is the consultant's familiarity with a particular company's personnel, machinery, or other unique variables specific to the assignment that might otherwise impact the success of the project. If a prospective client is envisioning having to spend additional time explaining organizational structures, formal and informal power bases within the company, company history, cultural relevancies, the industry, and the equipment or personnel to the consultant, then the time invested in that effort might not be quantitatively captured. All this might make a lower fee quote look a lot less attractive to a prospect than a higher fee from an experienced and knowledgeable consultant who has worked with the company or is familiar with the company's unique aspects. This expertise forms the basis of what many former employees can offer a previous employer and allows former employees to compete effectively for their business. The former employee has the advantage over other consultants because he or she does not require "ramp-up time" to learn the business or need to have the nuances of the company and its products, competition, and consumers or customers explained.

This criterion can also be turned on its head at times, and a prospect or client might determine that they do *not* want someone with prior experience with the company because that person might be perceived as being "tainted" and therefore not objective. Again, depending on the project requirements and the solution being sought, the criterion might be judged differently on a project-by-project basis.

Multiple location accessibility. One last criterion that some prospects might highly value is the need to provide consulting services in multiple locations either simultaneously, or at other times, across different cultures and in far-flung international cities. If a prospect has international locations and is part of a multinational corporation, the need to conduct a consulting assignment with sensitivities to different cultures, or to have enough members on a consulting project team to "blanket" multiple locations concurrently, or to have experience in multinational projects might be of paramount importance. In my own consulting practice, the ability to either provide simultaneous translation services to non-native English-speaking client employees, assist clients in replacing an outdated computer system with minimal data loss or downtime (referred to as "cutover training") across multiple locations, or staff consulting teams to provide consistent training across far-reaching regional offices has often been a determining factor in whether we received an assignment or not.

Selecting a Consultant Checklist

1. Have you determined what success would look like and can you communicate it to others?
2. Can you identify what level of expertise you require?
3. Do you know how you will assess the "fit" of various consulting organizations with your stated needs?
4. Have you confirmed and checked the references provided (or even asked for them)?
5. Do you know what your budget for the project is and how that will impact or affect your deliberations on which consultant to choose?
6. Have you sourced consultants who are appropriate for the business opportunity from multiple sources (word of mouth, publications, industry associations, etc.)?

Contracting with a Consultant

Key Learning Points:

- The importance of contracting for consulting services
- What is to be included in a contract or agreement
- What a Request For Proposal (RFP) entails
- Various ways to determine how a consultant is to be compensated
- The evaluative criteria used to measure success
- How to structure fees
- How to clarify the scope of the project

When you say that you agree to a thing in principle you mean that you have not the slightest intention of carrying it out.

—Prince Otto Eduard Leopold von Bismarck-Schonhausen

To this point in the process, you, as the client, have determined that your needs are best met with a consultant's assistance, have determined what criteria are most important in assessing the consultant you will ultimately select, and are now focused on how to formalize the arrangement and officially establish a contract with the consultant. For many clients and also consultants, this is the most difficult and uncomfortable part of the relationship and the facet they both at times wish they could avoid completing. Of course, this is also the first place both will run to when issues arise during the course of the assignment and the understandings that one side had believed were clearly agreed to turn out to be less certain and mutually acceptable to the other party.

Importance of Contracting

Consulting and contracting for consultative assistance is first and foremost a service business. Unlike businesses that produce a "product" that is easily defined, described, identified, and measurable (be it to certain standards of strength, color, functionality, etc.), consulting services are often more nebulous and difficult to define in many assignments. The output of the engagement between client and consultant might take on many forms and is more difficult to quantify.

Some consultants and clients will claim that this difficulty is what makes contracts nearly superfluous. Owing to the complexity of the arrangement, neither side will push too hard for a formal agreement and will jump past it right to conducting the actual assignment or work to be done. Of course, as long as there is some understanding of what the fee will be and for how long it is to be paid, everything else is deemed to be mere details and not worth the effort. For example, in dealing with one of my clients, the primary contact was not very interested in performing the role of contract administrator, and so he found every excuse to not do the necessary due diligence on the contractual aspect of the project. Being eager to work with the client and not wanting to lose business on something as meaningless as a contract when I had an agreement in principle with the client contact, I began the project. But when the project I had initially assumed I was working on grew to include many other ancillary tasks and I was alerted midway through the project that the funding to pay for my services was not authorized, I called a halt to the project. While I learned a very important lesson about contracting from a consultant's perspective, the client also was equally impacted because of the time and effort expended with no results to show for it, and she lost face internally as a result.

The other side of the coin has clients and consultants becoming so focused on the formality of the contract, that they lose sight of the original intent of the project. This rigidity has led to almost comical outcomes in my consulting practice. In one instance, I was asked to help a Marketing department build a "sales story" that could be used by salespeople to help them sell against a particular competitor that had been gaining market share. Unbeknownst to the Marketing department, the company was acquiring the same competitor in an acquisition simultaneous to the project initiative. Although the prudent thing might have been to refocus the project on creating a "selling story" that built on the new found synergies of the acquisition, we were told to adhere to the contract as written, even though the output was never read, presented to management, or used in any way once created.

Another time, I was called in to a company to help develop training for a particular piece of software that was to be used to assist the Marketing and Sales departments in analyzing opportunities. The contract called for a pilot or test of the training materials prior to rolling it out more broadly to the entire training population. Even though a decision was reached midway through the project to change vendors and applications and no longer implement the original piece of software, I was asked to complete the original training according to the design as stipulated in the contract for software that was no longer being used by the company and was no longer relevant to the needs of the organization (but the contract mandated it, so it *had* to be done).

The whole notion of establishing a contract strikes some as being overly formal and bound up in legalese that causes nothing but good agreements to go bad as the two parties wrangle back and forth to get the clauses of the contract approved by a legal department that is not familiar with, or even impacted by, the agreement. There is some kernel of truth in certain instances of corporate attorneys performing the role of "deal breakers" under the shield of protecting the interests of the firm they represent and unnecessarily preventing a well-intentioned and positively motivated project from moving forward because of misunderstandings or misapplication of their role as legal counsel.

However, it has been my experience that if the client and the consultant are truly aligned with each other on the project's breadth, depth, scope, etc., the contract is more a formality than a huge undertaking.

In my consulting practice, I even avoid the word *contract* as much as possible, preferring to use the term *agreement* in its place. Most business people are comfortable conferring on an agreement and working jointly to craft out an agreement that is mutually satisfactory to both parties. However, once the agreement is referred to as a "contract," it then often becomes imperative that each side reach for their legal counsel to ensure that they are not being taken advantage of in the contract. The fact that a contract is an agreement and nothing more than that still does not prevent this phenomenon from occurring. The agreement should stipulate the following:

- Date the project will begin and end (either by completion of an event or a specific future date)
- What each party will provide to the other (the most typical being level of payment in exchange for specified services)
- What is included as part of the fee and what is outside the fee (for example, expenses)
- Signature of acceptance and agreement to the aforementioned

As long as your agreement stipulates these specifics, then you, in essence, have a contract without having to raise the fears of entering into a "contract." (While this might not be a legal definition, it has served me well in working with clients over time.)

A contract or agreement that is written and formally signed and agreed to by both parties is extremely important, if for no other reason than it forces both parties to document their expectations and objectives, and express their intentions to each other. A project that is so ill defined that it eludes the parties' ability to document it in an agreement or a contract will never meet with success for either party. By virtue of going through the exercise of agreeing to a contract, both the consultant and the client are better able to synthesize what the project is to accomplish and how that is to be done.

Verbal contracts are legally binding and can be used between clients and consultants, but have the added pressure of being subject to interpretation by each party and remembered differently (even if done honestly and not with an intent to unilaterally modify the agreement). For that reason, it is not advised that contracts be created based solely on a verbal conversation. As a rule, I always follow up with at minimum an e-mail repeating the understanding of the project as I know it, and asking the client to respond back with their approval of my synopsis. Whether this would stand up in a court or not is not as strong a motivator for me to do this as wanting the client to participate in structuring the agreement.

Given that consulting and contracting for consulting is still a very relationship-specific endeavor that is dependent on the trust one has with the other, the agreement or contract is really more an effort to create a mutually defined project and payment schedule than to ensnare the other party in a legal loophole. It is because of this that many consultants are rather reluctant to bring legal action against a client. While the consultant might even be "right" in a legal sense, the victory would be short lived as the end result of that "Pyrrhic victory" would be the spreading of the word that the consultant sues clients, and with that news would come fewer and fewer assignments as clients would be loathe to contract with that consultant. I will give you two examples of this from my own experience.

My business partner, Jeff Clow, and I had completed some work for a major consumer packaged goods company that was to be paid for at the conclusion of the project. This firm was looking to make their year-end results look more favorable to Wall Street. They decided to hold off on all vendor payments due in the fourth quarter until January of the following year so that it would appear that their cash position was stronger than it really might have been. Now, while I hold no illusions that our contract was the difference between their appearing profitable and not to Wall Street, we got caught in the decision that impacted *all* vendors. After numerous and repeated phone calls and e-mails to follow up on where our payment was, we finally reached our client contact (a lower-level manager who was likely instructed to avoid our calls, but got trapped by picking up the phone at the wrong time and found us calling at that moment). After explaining that this is how we make our living and that they were not fulfilling their end of the agreement, we not only did not receive payment when expected (we saw that check in mid-January), we also were told that we were difficult to do business with and that we were no longer able to work with this particular company.

In another instance with another company, I had struck a multi-phase deal with a contact, and as an incentive to have the client fulfill the entire contract, I provided a reduced fee on the condition that they complete all phases. Should they stop midway, a higher per-phase cost would be owed to us. In essence, it was a volume discount: Use our services for the first five phases, and the sixth is at a much-reduced fee rate. Well, as often happens, the original client contact left the company in mid-project. The person assigned to take that person's place had a different perspective on priorities and did not want to complete the project's remaining phases. When I pointed out that the project would actually be *more* expensive to stop at this point than to complete, since there would be higher per-phase costs associated with the project, the new client contact balked and wanted to renegotiate at that point. Even here, when I had the law on my side, but certainly did not want to lose a good client and had to factor in the value of winning this minor battle over losing the client's entire future business, I still offered to forfeit the remaining amount and in essence rip up the contract. Although I thought I was bending over backwards to accommodate the new client contact and to get off on the right foot with him, he has not done any further business with us and has let it be known that he will not because he objected to our including a clause in the original contract (that he did not see, or sign, or was even a part of the agreement, yet it had been passed through their legal department) that "mandated" that he would have to pay for something he did not want. Obviously, I check the business press frequently to see if he has been given some other assignment or has moved on to another company so that I can be sure to send him a congratulatory note!

The RFP Process

In some instances (typically in large companies and governmental agencies), a client might request that consulting firms complete a Request For Proposal (RFP) as a response to an identified project need. Depending on the organization that is soliciting these RFPs, there is often a desire to keep the process as fair as possible and make the decision on which consultant is awarded the project on objective criteria. For this reason, RFPs are often collected with identifying information removed from the response so that no one knows which company submitted which response, other than an identifier number. The sponsoring organization will typically require at least three bids to be received to ensure that the decision has been made only after a compare-and-contrast review of more than a single vendor's proposal.

At its core, this is a very reasonable and above-board way to approach the selection of consultants. Put your best proposal in front of the decision makers (be it based on price, creativity, comprehensiveness, match of solution to stated problem, etc.) and allow the objective process to make the final determination.

To further make it seem above board, there will often be no opportunity to clarify understanding of the document that the consultants respond to and everyone has the same chance to interpret it. This interpretation then becomes part of the evaluation criteria: Did the consultant understand what we need? In some instances, there will be an open meeting for *all* vendors expressing an interest in responding to the RFP to attend where all can ask questions and hear answers. Again, all have the same access to the information, and no one has an unfair advantage over another vendor.

Now, not to cast aspersions on the process unduly, but it is not always what it seems at first blush. On its surface, it appears to create a level playing field where everyone has an equal chance of responding and winning. I have found the reality in some instances is much less objective.

- The criteria used to evaluate the proposals can be slanted toward a particular vendor's strengths (the weighting provided to "previous work experience with this department" can effectively knock out any other competitors who might be rather competent, but have no work experience with that department).
- It is not unheard of for the preferred consultant to actually create the RFP on behalf of the client and do so in a way that minimizes any vendor from gaining a foothold in the account without their involvement.* The preferred vendor can limit access to the RFP process by distributing the RFP only to those who will agree to work with them as co-consultants, thereby ensuring that no

---

*For an excellent example of this, I suggest reading *Soldier of Fortune 500: A Management Survival Guide for the Consulting Wars* by Steve Romaine, Prometheus Books, Amherst, NY, 2002.

matter which company wins, the preferred consultant will remain on the project.

- The timing of when RFPs are sent out and when the response must be received can ensure that few, if any, unprepared consultants can respond. Only the consultants who had a previous warning that this was to occur can reply in time. The client company would conclude that the other vendors had an opportunity to bid, but passed due to lack of interest, lack of expertise, or some other reason, and therefore, the decision must be made without their involvement.

I have been involved in a few RFPs over the years and have walked away and refused to respond to a good many more than I have replied. I have an inherent distrust of the objectivity of the process, and unless I am allowed access to ask questions (either publicly or in private) about the RFP, I refuse to do all the work required to reply (and it is typically an arduous and involved process) only to become "cannon fodder" or the vendor used to compare the preferred vendor against before offering the job to the preferred vendor.

In actuality, this worked in my favor one time. I had been solicited to respond to an RFP, and after reviewing it, I decided it was not likely to be as fair a decision as I would have hoped. I responded that I was withdrawing my name from consideration and would not be submitting a response. The client organization became nervous because their policy required that they have three vendors to compare, and with my dropping out of the process, they were in jeopardy of not being able to award the project to anyone because the process could not move forward without vendors to use for comparison (even if the comparison was really a charade). They called me and asked me to reconsider. I said I would, but only under the condition that I be allowed to interview three executives (and I specified by job title which executives) prior to the response in order to get a better handle on the needs. They relaxed the rule about no contact with us prior to submission of reply, and as a result of my interviews, I was able to change the criteria of how to best select a consultant to meet the newly developed needs. I did not ultimately get the project, but took comfort in making the original consulting firm sweat a bit.

You as a client might be mandated by corporate policy or might even prefer to use an RFP process to ensure objectivity. Be forewarned though that consultants have been known to go "over the head" of the client contact for these decisions and curry favor with a more-senior executive to ensure the project is skewed that consultant's way.

Different Approaches

Contracting for consulting services can take many different forms and is constrained only by the imagination of the two parties striking the deal and their willingness to be bound by the approach suggested. There is no "right way" to contract for services beyond the legal issues of what constitutes a formal agreement and whether there is appropriate consideration being offered for services rendered. In this instance, "appropriate" does not mean the amount or the value of payment, but the "type" of payment. For example, offering to trade your adolescent daughter for two customer satisfaction surveys and a findings report is *not* considered appropriate consideration.

Some of the more commonly used approaches to establishing contractual terms are as follows:

- **Retainer.** A retainer is a fee agreed upon that covers work to be completed within a specified period of time. Retainers may be used instead of the "pay-as-you-go" model when it is anticipated that a consultant will be required to provide assistance on multiple projects over the given time period. Occasionally, the consulting work will be limited to certain tasks or a certain level of utilization, such as hours a week or number of consultants on site.

  Benefits: Both the client and the consultant can take comfort in the fact that an agreement is in place and that they will not have to worry about creating a specific agreement for each of a series of small projects. This approach is often less expensive for the client, and allows the consultant to bundle services, offer discounted rates, and minimize their own concerns about cash flow.

  Detractions: Since retainers are generally given for currently unidentified projects, the potential for misalignment of expectations between the client and consultant exists. Also, the motivation to perform at their best might not be in place with a consultant who has a guaranteed income stream.

- **Flat fee.** In a flat fee scenario, the consultant offers to provide services at a previously determined fixed fee and does not charge incrementally for individual components of the project. In this scenario, the price is predetermined, and therefore the client does not pay based on the number of days a project lasts, amount of work to be done within the project's parameters, or number of people involved in the project.

Benefits: The benefits to the client are that the costs are known up front and can be budgeted for ahead of time. There are no surprises or unexpected bills showing up at the last minute, and no decisions have to be made about changing the project's scope due to a phase of the project consuming more of the allotted budget than anticipated.

Detractions: The negatives to this approach are that the project might become somewhat inflexible. A consultant might not be willing to provide additional value since it won't increase the project fee, and a client runs the risk of feeling they are not getting the best effort of the consultant because the fee is predetermined and there might be less inherent motivation to exceed beyond the anticipated results of the project.

- **Day rate.** A consultant who charges on a day rate basis is essentially selling time. The value or worth of the consultation is directly tied to the duration of the effort expended to complete the project. Often, consultants who charge day rates will provide any of the services they offer for the same scheduled rate per day. In this instance, the consultant offers to do work of the client's choosing at the same fees.

Benefits: The client and the consultant can manage the budgetary aspects of the relationship to ensure that it is closely monitored. A consultant is able to plan their work around the number of days required to complete the project, and the client has a sense that they are getting the effort required to complete the project within an agreed-upon time frame.

Detractions: The client and the consultant measure the effort expended, but do not focus on the results in this approach. Is a consultant who works more quickly deserving of the punishment of lesser fees because the work is completed more quickly? Is time devoted to a project really an indicator of contribution? Is the unspoken motivation for some consultants to string a project out longer to acquire more fees?

My business partner, Jeff Clow, was formerly my immediate supervisor at a company we were affiliated with in the 1990s. One of my peers at that firm would often comment ad nauseum on how hard he worked and how much work he was doing. Jeff would calmly remind him that his having to work as hard as he did, while appreciated, was not something that was worthy of reward by itself; the rewards were due to those who produced results. Seeing as how others were able to produce results that surpassed the alleged harder worker's levels with fewer hours invested on project work, his long hours were more likely a sign that the time being spent was unproductive time and, rather than being rewarded, was worthy of corrective action.

- **Per "x."** In this approach, the project is defined in terms of "how many" of something occurs. Whether it is based on how many attendees participate in the workshop, or how many people are interviewed and then aggregated as part of a larger study, or some other quantifiable measure of activity and productivity, the determinant of the fee is based on number of occurrences.

Benefits: The benefits are similar to the above "day rate" in that the budget can be carefully controlled ("Only interview 7, not 10 people," or "We will cap the class at 12 and not have all 20 managers attend a session"). In instances where the project value can be easily calculated by such a strict quantitative approach, it might work well for both consultant and client.

Detractions: Many projects do not lend themselves to such simple quantifiable calculations. Do we choose to ignore the input of one departmental executive because it costs too much to include the person in a survey? Is the value of the workshop and the content irrespective of attendees present (and this is quite debatable, depending on situation and perspective)?

- **Barter.** The barter approach trades one service for another. A client in the information services industry might swap product or assistance in establishing a management information system to track manufacturing processes, financial reporting, sales, etc., in exchange for a consultant's offering of new product introduction assistance. Rather than exchange money as consideration, there is an exchange of services.

  Benefits: If you find opportunity to provide a quid pro quo exchange, this can be rather beneficial (though, I would strongly suggest you check with your accountant as to how to track and report that transaction for tax purposes) and might accomplish both parties' needs.

  Detractions: The obvious downside is the rarity with which there can be a fair trade between businesses that offer different services. Also, depending on accounting practices, there might be additional requirements for documenting the value of the bartered services.

- **Tied to business results.** As of late, there has been an increase in consultants offering to place their fee or a portion thereof on the success of the initiative or consulting project within the client company. In this approach, the client pays the consultant based on corporate performance at some predetermined future point.

  Benefits: This approach appears to be intrinsically motivating for the client and consultant to ensure that the means provided to the end result clearly address the specified needs. The consultant is at jeopardy to lose (or stands to gain) a portion of the fee and therefore will provide their best effort to ensure success and higher fee payment.

  Detractions: The intuitive approach of linking the consultant's efforts to the client's success and thereby creating a sense of "we are all in this together" might have a very nonintuitive outcome. The consultant is *not* responsible for the actions of the client and cannot dictate to the client what to do, how to do it, when to do it, etc. The consultant is now further driven by the very short-term outcome of securing the remainder of the fee that had been held back and, therefore, might make suggestions that are very short-term focused and are not in the best interests of the client longer term. As someone who has been both consultant and client at points in my career, I can share that this approach, while well-intentioned, has many issues that would need to be addressed up front. Failure to do so will result in lots of finger pointing and accusations about who is to blame when things do not go as planned.

- **Partial ownership.** Related to the two prior approaches is the exchange of consultation support for a "piece of the company." Rather than receive payment for consulting services, the consultant trades services for stock or ownership of the client company. This approach was seen occasionally with cash-strapped dot.com-type businesses that required assistance, but could not afford to absorb the cash flow impact of paying for consulting during start-up.

  Benefits: The link between the performance of the company and the consultant's efforts is clear. The consultant has reason to provide their best effort here because it will pay off in ownership value.

  Detractions: The same detractions apply here in that the consultant is in a gray area of being part advisor to the company and part employee or owner, and as such, the objectivity of recommendations might be colored by the matrix view of self-interested gain. Crossing the line from independent advisor to owner dredges up conflicts of interest that can at times prevent clarity of thought and maintenance of appropriate roles (either as owner or as consultant to the company).

- **Value received.** In a value received approach to contracting for consulting services, the benefit of the consulting is determined based on its inherent worth and not effort expended. To make this more concrete conceptually: Do any of us really care if a heart surgeon takes 15 minutes or 15 hours as long as we are confident that our surgery was handled professionally and competently? Would we value the 15-hour surgery more than the 15-minute one if the same end result was provided—additional quality of life?

Benefits: The focus is where it needs to be in this instance. Consulting should be based on results and not on effort or days or numbers of discrete steps taken to reach that outcome. The value of the project to the client will be determined individually by that client.

Detractions: The problem with this approach is that the seemingly same project will have different values to different clients. A consultant will charge one client one fee, and another client a different fee for what appears to be the same level or quantity of work. Should clients ever talk with one another and compare notes, it might lead to a significant issue for the consultant. This is also why some clients resort to the other approaches that rely on quantitative or measurable outputs as the foundation for fee structures. At least each client knows that they are getting the market value of a consultant's time, or number of interviews, etc.

Obviously, some projects might use a hybrid or mixed approach that uses more than one approach to the total project fee (establishing the minimum and maximum number of interviews to be conducted, capping the class at 18, and establishing a fixed price for the entire project).

Establishment of Objectives

From the perspective of the consultant trying to sell services to a prospect or client, whenever possible, I will look to change the dynamic away from a discussion around the commodity aspect of the consulting project and toward the business issue being addressed. Rather than address how many days I will invest in the project, how many people I will interview, or how many attendees will participate in a training session I conduct, I attempt to raise the discussion to the business benefit of the project's successful completion. The value of a well-researched strategic planning document is infinitely more valuable than a report that is sold as the output of ten interviews of senior executives and some analysis of the industry.

When I propose to conduct a training program for a client, I am not selling the number of manuals I produce, the number of computer-generated slides I create, or the quantity of exercises I provide. I am selling a competency that I will assist their participants in developing. The worth and value of that is more highly treasured than the value of the manual or of my time to present the material (Do I really want to be in the business of determining the cost of a workshop based on the costs of ink, copy paper, binders, tabs, etc.? And, does my client truly want to make a decision on which consultant to choose based on which one has the most efficient deal with office supply centers to purchase materials at cost?).

The issue in getting into the "price wars" around consulting services is the effort of some clients and consultants to apply a price to effort and not results received. Just as the fellow consultant used to whine to Jeff Clow about how difficult it was to keep afloat with all the work being produced, clients who focus on the days/time/participants to be impacted often miss the more important business-building objectives that should be fueling the effort. What is to be accomplished and what is the worth to the business to have the initiative succeed is a much more relevant variable for determining consultant fees.

What this approach also clarifies is that no two projects are ever alike and, therefore, cannot be truly compared side by side. Two companies will out of necessity approach projects differently and will have varying importance assigned to projects according to the project's impact on the overarching strategic goal for that company.

Rather than get rigidly tied to the means of the project (days worked on the project, interview targets, classes held, etc.), addressing the project from the perspective of what is the desired outcome and what consultant can best provide the tools or assistance to accomplish that outcome will provide a stronger consultant-client relationship and will make the contracting for consulting services easier (everyone understands the purpose and the value of the project and how to achieve it becomes less an issue of contentiousness and more a cooperative venture).

Determine Outcomes

The desired outcome of the consulting project might be quantitative or qualitative. Examples of quantitative outcomes are:

- Reducing errors from 3 per 1,000 transactions to 1.5 per 1,000 transactions
- Increasing "close rates" for first sales calls from 5 percent to 15 percent within a year
- Improving pricing levels to increase profit by 4 percent without a corresponding drop in volume
- Reduce absenteeism by 10 percent within the next six months

Examples of qualitative outcomes are:

- Improve customer satisfaction on a 5-point scale from 2.2 to 4.0 (even though this is a measurement and quantified, it is still a qualitative measurement based on what is being measured)
- Increase employee understanding of how their actions impact corporate profitability
- Understand the causes of employee turnover so that a retention plan can be developed
- Identify how vendors and suppliers can more efficiently provide input into our manufacturing processes

Regardless of which of the above objectives is chosen to pursue, quantitative or qualitative, the methods used to accomplish them would be far less important than the successful achievement of the outcome or objective pursued. When seen in this light, discussions on whether to conduct telephone surveys or face-to-face interviews become secondary to awarding the project to consultants who understand the issues and are willing to be held accountable for providing the appropriate insights and consultative assistance.

Evaluative Criteria

In discerning the appropriateness of a consultant's proposal or contract to meet a project's needs, one of the tools frequently relied upon is the criteria used to evaluate or assess the initiative's success. A well-managed project will include within it the criteria required to judge its success. A poorly proposed or contracted project will have open-ended criteria or no criteria specified at all.

Given that many projects are multi-phased and at times require conformance to tight time frames, it might be appropriate to use very quantitative criteria in assessing the project's success.

Quantitative

Dates met. Did the project, or any phase within it, meet the desired date established? A project that is designed to address a competitor's actions in the marketplace must be timely, or the opportunity to respond will be lost. In those instances, or similar situations, timing is of the essence. A well-run project in all other factors that does not meet the time consideration is a project that will not be effective.

Interviews conducted. If a project is to gain the insights of different executives, customers, or others with unique points of view, it is essential that the interviews occur as planned. Failure to conduct the interviews required will result in a final report that is either jaded, skewed toward one perspective or another, or at minimum, incomplete.

People trained. Related to the above, if a training session is to be conducted for the sales force, and only three-quarters of the sales force is exposed to the training, that will severely hamper the success of the program. In those instances, it is recommended that all those impacted be exposed to the new process, training, tool, or software exposure, etc.

Qualitative

Satisfaction measures. One of the more commonly used measures in evaluating a consulting assignment's impact on the organization or individual targeted to receive the benefit of the consulting is a satisfaction measure. As any veteran of classroom-style training sessions has likely endured, at the end of the session, an evaluation form is passed out and participants are asked to complete an evaluation that is either a rank order, check the box corresponding to your feeling or rating, or in some instances open-ended questions requiring a narrative response. As often happens, this exercise is done as people are gathering up their stuff to make the next meeting, run to make connections for shared car rides or air travel schedules, etc. Furthermore, the person who has just been exposed to the consultative assistance is not always in the best position to judge the merits of that assistance. Oftentimes, the person has not had time to implement the suggestions, is struggling with the transition from doing it the previous way to the newly instructed way, or might be wrestling with their own issues ("I don't belong in this training; I am a good worker already," or "Why do I have to do it this way? It worked perfectly fine the other way and I knew what to do before—now I am all confused," etc.).

Level of awareness. Another commonly used qualitative measure used to evaluate consulting projects is level of awareness. Some consulting projects are not designed to re-organize tasks within a department or provide specific tactical assistance at all. Rather, the purpose of the consulting is to raise people's awareness of a situation or educate them on the perils of ignoring a potential outcome. This kind of consultation is difficult to truly assess. How do you really know if someone is aware of something? Typically, it is assumed that if someone attended a session where the topic is discussed, and perhaps signed a document acknowledging that they attended and are aware or versed in what was presented, then the person *must* be aware of the content.

It has been my experience that Diversity in the Workplace and Sexual Harassment are topics that have typically been handled this way. The strong assumption is that if a person has been exposed to the information and indicates that they heard it and understood the material presented, then they have acquired sufficient awareness to make the right decisions and choices. While this might be a legally defensible position that protects companies from certain forms of litigation, its effectiveness at preventing the situations that caused the need for the consultation in the first place might be subject to further discussion.

Structuring Fees

As a client, you might not be aware that savvy consultants will attempt to configure the payment schedule in ways that benefit them, or at least confirm that the prospect is a viable business opportunity. From a consultant's perspective, there are few things more frustrating and disheartening than working with a contact at a prospect to create a project plan, only to find out that the contact does not control the decision making for the project and/or there is not sufficient budget to accommodate the project's costs. Seasoned consultants will quickly attempt to root out the "contenders" from the "pretenders" so as not to invest too much time in projects that have no hope of being funded.

One of the techniques used by consultants is to ask for start-up money or an up-front payment to "seal the deal." What the consultant is accomplishing by doing this is:

- Confirming your level of commitment to move ahead. Only a client that was really interested in completing the project would invest up front in a project.
- Providing the client with motivation to complete the project, the thinking being that there is already an investment in the project, so it is not prudent business to cancel it midway.
- Covering business costs that the consultant will assume in the execution of the project (for example, air travel or purchases made on behalf of the project) that might not be reimbursed at all, or perhaps will be reimbursed on a time delay, and therefore, the consultant is protecting their own cash flow.
- Using the assumed belief in "fairness" to an advantage to prevent future legal issues.

In my consulting practice, I ask for partial payment at the onset of the project. If there is no up-front payment, the client might feel that the project can be cancelled without jeopardy since no "tangible" work has been done. My perspective on this is that I have done work and just have not been paid for it to that point. I had to prepare for the call(s), I had to create a proposal, I had to meet or speak with various people, I perhaps made a presentation, etc. While on the one hand, these are my internal marketing costs or costs of doing business, they also need to be recouped when a project is signed. I am willing to absorb those costs when a project is not forthcoming, but as soon as I do sign a project agreement, I want to recover those costs for that project up front.

Psychologically, when a project has been partially paid for up front, it removes the desire to possibly cut it too quickly. Since there is already forward motion or inertia on the project and there has been money exchanged, the project has the perception of being further along than it might truly be and, therefore, should be seen through to its completion.

As mentioned before, as a consultant, I have invested in the business opportunity ahead of securing the project and, therefore, want to be paid for that effort. Additionally, I might incur expenses related to the project as part of project research (purchasing competitive products for comparison, air travel to meet with subject-matter experts in the company's remote offices, etc.). These expenses can be more easily accommodated if I have been paid a portion of the fee up front. Otherwise, I would need to get checks cut from the client for expenses as they occur, which, more times than not, slows down the process greatly.

The last bullet in the list points to the precarious posture the consultant must maintain in client relationships. It is the rare consultant who will ever sue a client for early cancellation of a project or for some issue related to client non-performance. While it does occur, the downside is vast. A consultant who sues a client will quickly run the risk of being labeled as a consultant that no client wishes to do business with in the future. If a consultant has received payment up front and has structured the contract so that less money is due toward the end of the contract (regardless of when the actual work is to be done or completed), the exposure or risk is minimized. The consultant is never in a position of having done more work than has been paid for to date. This is what I was attempting to do with the earlier example of providing a lesser-cost workshop only after the first few had been done: I was paid a higher percentage of the money earlier in the contract and could offer a much-reduced fee for the remaining workshop delivery.

It is sometimes smart business practice for the consultant to offer an incentive for the client to undertake a larger scale project than they otherwise might have chosen to do on their own. This is not to say that the consultant suggests phases to the consulting project that are inappropriate or tries to "pad the bill" with unnecessary components. Rather, the consultant might bundle additional services into a consulting proposal that are entirely appropriate and justified, but would not be budgeted or supportable had that component been proposed on its own. For example, I am in the middle of a discussion with a client as I write this book *either* to develop a training workshop or to provide some industry trend perspective/strategic-planning assistance. It is my suggestion that we fold the two together and use the attendees as part of the strategic-planning research that will be necessary. So, instead of using a half day to train the executives and then releasing them back to their jobs, I proposed that we keep them for a full day and facilitate a strategic-planning session during the afternoon of that day. In this way, I can offer a price that includes both components, but is still less than they would absorb if they were to contract with me for each separately. My incentive to this client is to maximize the use of the time we will all be together to accomplish both objectives, at a consulting fee that is more preferable than if they were to hire me or anyone else for each project independently. My "win" is that I am providing additional services and value for a higher fee than I would have otherwise commanded. The client benefits by getting both projects for the fee of roughly one and a half.

Contractual Necessities

When contracting with consultants for project work, scoping out the details of the project might be the hardest and most crucial step of the contracting step, but if you as a client take your eye off the ball or assume too much, you might be surprised by some of the other unexpected tricks that occur.

For instance, it is not at all uncommon for a more-senior member of a consulting organization to sell the project and lead you as the client to believe that the consulting firm is prepared to provide the best and brightest for the assignment. The natural assumption is often that the person who sold the project to you will be the person who works on the project. After all, who knows the unique context of the project and the specifics about the personnel better than the person who has worked to sell its benefits to you? Unfortunately, it is not at all uncommon for there to be a "bait and switch" of sorts. The partner or more-senior level consultant sells the project and might even commit to being available for the presentations back to the most senior management within your company, but the actual day-to-day work will be done by lower-level and often less-experienced consultants. These consultants might be learning their craft on your project and might just represent the consultants who were previously unassigned to more glamorous assignments within the consulting organization. This leaves you stuck with lesser-skilled and less-desirable consultants who are learning about your industry, your company, and the specifics about the assignment's requirements—all while you are stuck paying for assistance you had assumed was to be much more senior and much more comprehensive. Of course, the partner will return when it is time to make a presentation because that is often a chance to sell the next project.

As a client, it is essential that you specify who will work on your project or require that you get to meet and refuse anyone from the consulting organization prior to their being assigned to the team. If possible, you might want to make it a clause in the contract that the person selling the project to you *must* also work on it (though, you might run the risk of having a consultant assigned to the team who does not want to be there, which can lead to other issues mid-project).

Milestones or go/no-go steps are another critical component of contracting that wise clients will look to include. In the event that circumstances change, priorities are shifted, or a whole host of other outcomes and eventualities do occur, it is smart business to include periodic check points to determine if the project still makes as much sense to pursue as it did initially. When this is combined with the over-lapping fee structure, a smart client can protect his or her interests and not be "upside down" on the balance between project fee and propor-tion of project completed.

By including these mutually agreed-upon points in the project's progression, there is also a subtle pressure applied to the consultant to make sure that there is no lag in productivity or performance, as any hiccup in the process might lead to you as the client pulling the plug on the project and dooming it to an earlier-than-planned termination.

Agreeing on the scope of the project is something that continues to bewilder even the best consultant and client relationships if not addressed up front and forthrightly. From the consultant's vantage point, clarity of scope is a necessity to prevent the client from continuing to pile on additional requirements or segments to the project. The consultant wants to protect the resources of his or her company (time to devote to projects, intellectual property, other consultants, etc.) and ensure that those resources are applied productively and profitably. As much of the estimates on how complex or how long a particular project will turn out to be is based on a mix of experience, guesswork, and the ability to define the project's boundaries up front, agreeing to and specifying the scope of the project is of paramount importance to the consultant.

Similarly, the scope of the project is of equal importance to the client. No client wants to "buy a pig in a poke" and be surprised when what they thought they were buying turns out to be a whole lot less than what they actually receive in the way of services and consultation. As a client, it is imperative that you reach some clearly spelled out list of expectations and requirements that the consultant will meet in the execution of the project.

The project should be specifically defined so that there is no confusion as to whether "x" is part of the expectation or not. If a client has to wonder, "Does the project also include 'y'?" or if a consultant worries, "Am I obligated to also perform 'z'?" then the scope is not properly documented, and the confusion, finger pointing, and invectives being hurled back and forth shall begin.

Given that consulting assignments are often based on developing competitive advantage or hoping to respond to a market situation in a way that leverages an opportunity, it is typically in the best interests of the client to demand that the consultant sign and agree to a confidentiality clause that prevents the consultant from sharing any information with anyone who is not involved in the project. It is for this reason that I will very often destroy files, programs, reports, etc., received from clients as part of the project upon completion of the project. It is safer for me as the consultant and it should be a mandatory requirement from the client to either return or destroy all documents, files, photos, etc., to prevent them from being passed on to a competitor or anyone else.

Some clients include as part of their contracts a clause (or separate document in certain instances) referred to a Non-Disclosure Agreement or NDA. These agreements bind the parties to not discuss the project, nor anything else about the relationship between the two companies. Given the competitive nature of many companies with regard to others in the marketplace, these agreements will occasionally extend to even forbidding the consultant from working for one of the client's competitors for a period of time after the project has been completed.

As a consultant, I am more than willing to adhere to those restrictions or ones that demand a "non-compete" clause (if I work for Pepsi on a project, I commit that I shall not work for Coca-Cola for a period of time), but for me to be exclusively a consultant for one company in a given industry or market niche will typically result in a higher consulting fee as I am at jeopardy of losing potential consulting revenue by not being permitted to approach certain companies. If your situation calls for that kind of "either it is us or them" ultimatum being delivered to your consultants, be prepared to pay for the privilege of exclusivity with that consultant.

Project Logistics

Depending on the needs of the project, there might be times when the specific logistics of where the work of the project will be completed become an issue. For projects that require consultants and internal employees to work side-by-side, it might be necessary to provide office space, telephone lines, computer equipment, temporary housing, or other logistical support to the consultants to ensure there is opportunity to maximize results. On other projects, one of the benefits of choosing to use a consultant over internal employees is that the project is self-contained and does not have to be completed on-site. In those instances, the consultant can complete the work in their office or even as they travel to and from other engagements if appropriate.

If the project entails access to proprietary computer systems or requires being able to get behind computer security systems or firewalls, then passwords, for example, will need to be issued so that the consultant can conduct the work necessary to complete the project. This would apply regardless of whether the work is done within the client's offices or from remote locations. In some instances where applications and access to information are available only within the intranet of the company, it will prove difficult to access information from outside the client location. Therefore, it is prudent to confirm what computer access the consultant will need to complete the project and ensure that if the work is to be completed from a location other than the client site, that there are no insurmountable obstacles to logging in to the systems to be used.

Another concern that you as a client might have in working with consultants concerns whether or not they are insured and what that insurance covers. When talking about insurance, there are typically two kinds that most often seem to apply to the client/consultant relationship.

The first refers to coverage that would handle personal injury, whether to the consultant or anyone who is injured as a result of the consultant's actions and efforts. I know that certain clients of mine have demanded that I sign a contract absolving them of responsibility for my actions that result in injury to me or others. Other times, I have had to provide proof of insurance to cover me in case of injuries while working either on their site or at my own office.

The second type of insurance that consultants will occasionally seek (and as a client, you might inquire about) is errors and omissions coverage, or E & O. In this coverage, should the advice of the consultant not be complete or should the counsel be followed and it turns out to be incorrect, an E & O policy would protect the consultant from having to pay a large settlement from savings or cash flow of the company in the event of being sued. Suing an individual consultant is a very rare occurrence, as the courts do not tend to put the onus of responsibility for a company's actions on the shoulders of anyone other than those of management of that firm. However, in the event that the consultant is judged to have been responsible for poor advice leading to disastrous results, some consultants have purchased this form of insurance. As with all matters related to insurance, law, and accounting, it is always best to seek independent expert opinion to ensure that your unique situation is properly understood and your interests are protected.

Logistically, the last thing you need to ensure is clearly understood by both internal employees and the consultant is the responsibility for managing the consultant while completing the project. If not told explicitly who within the client organization has responsibility for managing the project and, therefore, the consultant while working on the project, the consultant will quickly realize the person to please is the executive with budgetary control for the project. A consultant's natural inclination, not unlike anyone else's for that matter, is self-preservation. If the person signing the check is pleased, the likelihood of being considered for future projects is assumed to be strong. If forced to make a choice between pleasing a subject-matter expert within a company with no budget to spend, and a budget-controlling executive with limited expertise, the majority of consultants will see to it that the executive is kept happy.

Consultants will often attempt to get to as senior-level manager as they can during the course of the selling of the project or once on the assignment. A smart consultant will understand that more-senior executives likely have a greater span of control (including control over the budgets), and a generous consultant budget will typically reduce the chance of running into interference at the completion of the project (a consultant saying "Ms. Bigshot hired me to do this project, and I would suggest you take your concerns to her if you believe this is a poorly conceived idea" rarely leads to much further discussion from subordinates). Some middle-level executive clients will try to constrain their consultant into a very narrow window in an attempt to prevent that consultant from going over their head within the organization. The motivation for this is varied: In some instances, it is political ("This is my consultant and I am going to prevent anyone else from claiming him or her as their consultant"). Sometimes fear plays a role ("I don't know what I am doing, the consultant knows I am struggling, and I don't want management to be made aware of it"). Or power will sometimes be a motivator ("I sit at the side of the person who is making changes around here, and so as long as I am the one interacting with senior management to share results about the progress of the project, I am a more valuable employee. If I allow the consultant free access to the senior managers, I lose my base of power").

I can tell you that from my own experience, it is the rare middle-level employee who can prevent a determined consultant from gaining access to senior-level managers (unless the senior manager has specifically told the consultant *not* to provide updates directly, but to work through the client contact person). With the ease of voice mails, e-mails, copying a senior executive on correspondence, etc., it is rare when a consultant would not be able to establish contact with a senior executive. Remember, that consultant is running a business and has to make decisions that are in the best interests of the business; if left to his or her discretion, they will seek to speak to those who have the greatest opportunities to hire and provide budgets for project work. This is why it is critical that there be clear lines of communication with internal employees as to who has final authority on the consultant's work and what the chain of command is for project-related issues. If it is not spelled out and enforced, you cannot blame the consultant for following the trail of money up to a senior-level position.

Promotion

Upon occasion, owing to the uniqueness of a project, or to the importance of a project to the company's future strategic direction, or to the consultant's standing as an expert in the project's requirements, it might make sense to publicize the endeavor to the industry, customers, etc. Typically, this happens after the fact and often takes one of the following forms:

- Presentations to industry groups or association meetings
- Articles in trade publications
- A jointly developed advertisement

Obviously, both parties have to agree to do this, and there has to be appropriate clearances as to what can be shared publicly and what must remain confidential. The benefits of this are:

- Establishing market position
- Creating/reinforcing the image as innovative, efficient, or whatever the project was designed for
- Recruiting/retaining employees or selecting strategically vital employees who are identified as being important to the future of the company
- Communicating to customers that the company is addressing issues/meeting new needs/etc.

The synergies of aligning oneself with a market leader (or with a thought leader) and the instant recognition that comes with that can sometimes be more important than having to protect or hide the fact that the relationship exists between consultant and client. There is no shame in using a consultant for the overwhelming majority of projects, and with the proper message, it can be turned into a strong positive for either organization and oftentimes for both.

One caveat that I will share about this, though, is from my own personal experience when I first launched my firm. In my enthusiasm and excitement to gain some publicity for a recently completed successful project, I received permission from my client to distribute press releases to daily newspapers and industry publications related to my client's industry. I even went so far as to get approval on the content of the press release from my client before sending it out. One journalist in particular called me to get more details on the project (and I was only too happy to speak to the writer, as I envisioned terrific publicity was sure to follow). I ignored the bells going off in my head when the questions were all very negatively slanted: Is this company about to go under? Do you think they will lay people off this quarter? Why is it that their market position is slipping? I thought I adroitly handled each with a very positive reply and deflected those that were inappropriate for me to answer by suggesting that there were people within the client company who were better suited to reply to those questions. When the article appeared the following day, I had been misquoted, I had been made to appear to be rather critical of my client, and certain comments were fabricated and attributed to me! I had a devil of a time trying to explain that to the client, I assure you. Fortunately, the client was easily assuaged since they had similar experiences with this reporter and believed that I had *not* said what I was alleged to have said about them. The moral of the story though is when relying on journalists, you do not control the message. The independent nature of the coverage makes it often desirable (it has been endorsed by the writer, someone the reader knows and trusts), but it comes at the potential expense of the reporter not relaying the message as you would prefer. In an advertisement, you control the message. In a presentation, you control the message, with the possible exception of having to respond to questions, and even then, you choose how you answer, if you choose to answer, and what you choose to say to address the question. When seeking coverage in articles or providing quotes to writers, you can get burned because you do not control how it is going to be incorporated into a story theme. While this is relatively rare (most writers are ethical and are not looking to burn sources), it is a possible unintended outcome.

Checklist for Contracting with Consultants

1. Have you established the contractual terms with your consultant?
2. Have you chosen whether to use an RFP or not and do you have a rationale for choosing that approach? How rigorous will you be in keeping your decision based solely on responses and not allowing further contact?
3. What form of payment criteria will you use (based on value received, number of days of work, etc.)?
4. Do you have evaluative criteria for determining the success or failure of the project? Has the consultant been told that payment is related to the achievement of those objectives?
5. Has the fee structure been determined (partial payments, go/no-go steps, etc.)?
6. Is the scope of the project understood and aligned with the payment schedule in a way that makes sense for you? For the consultant?

Managing a Consultant

Key Learning Points:

- Importance of aligning expectations of skills, roles, and experience of the consultant with the project requirements
- Establishment of a communication protocol or process
- The necessity for mileposts and checkpoints within the project to confirm status
- Determination of how feedback is to be provided (and solicited), and how confidentiality is to be maintained
- Confirmation of scope and project parameters
- Selection of project team members and communicating their level of involvement and expectations of team members with them
- Ensuring that the consultant is clear on tolerance for soliciting other business within the company while on the project
- Ensuring that projects requiring multiple consultants are not unintentionally prevented from succeeding due to competing consultants vying for dominance

Igor Stravinsky was offered $4,000 to compose the music for a Hollywood film.
"It is not enough," he said.
"It's what we paid your predecessor," the producer said.
"My predecessor had talent," Stravinsky replied. "I have not, so for me the work is
more difficult."

Expectations

One of the most difficult aspects of working with consultants is navigating the fine line between over-managing the consultant and not providing enough management to ensure that the project is properly executed. Given that the consultant is not an internal employee subject to the same expectations and conventions that you might use with your own group, the issue becomes complex rather quickly. Compounding this phenomenon is the fact that the consultant is often assumed to have experiences that exceed your and your group's command of the subject matter of the project. The implications and ramifications of this often lead to poorly managed projects that produce unexpected results and to the ensuing finger pointing and claims of culpability and absolution from responsibility that are soon to follow.

Factors leading to this failure to achieve positive results are:

- Client believes that the consultant has more or deeper understanding of the issues, objectives, and project requirements than the consultant truly has.
- Consultant uses the lack of clarity about reporting structure, their independent status, and the perceived aura of being an expert to create a hands-off protocol for project management.
- Client perceives the consultant is beyond reproach or not even subject to being questioned. To blame or question the consultant would be a challenge to the client's process for hiring consultants. In this case, the client subscribes to the following: "We hired this consultant, and we can't now admit that they don't know how to do an element of the project correctly, so we shall accept what we are provided, choose to ignore it, and not admit that we made a mistake with this assignment."

- Client changes the parameters of the project so that the original scope of the project is no longer desirable or relevant to the newly formed objectives.

Content

Among the first things to consider when managing a consultant is the responsibility for developing the content of the project, whether it be a survey, a training workshop, a strategic session, etc. Some projects are best completed by the consultant providing direction, guidance, or perhaps a process (standard or customized) and the client then being required to complete the content development according to the consultant-provided standard.

This works best when the client is in possession of the specific components required to address the needs of the project, but might not be sure as to the best way to approach the project. Examples of this approach being used correctly are:

- **New item launches.** The consultant might provide the template for the effective introduction of a new item, but the client would ultimately have to provide strategic insights, competitive positioning, etc.
- **Proprietary data projects.** Those projects where the company's own data (sales information, pricing, profit, etc.) are incorporated into the project's completion would essentially result in the client having to provide significant input (or at the very minimum, access to that data).
- **Ideation sessions.** Upon occasion, a client might request a consultant to facilitate a discussion between executives, groups, or other factions that are not currently used to communicate with each other. In these sessions, the consultant might provide the tasks to generate and focus discussions, but would not be in a position to provide anything but facilitation support. The participants would be responsible for providing the different perspectives and ideas.

Other consulting projects are best served by the consultant providing the lion's share of the content, and oftentimes, the process as well. If the project is one where the client has minimal experience and is not in a position to properly provide input, it might be beneficial for the consultant to provide the content of the project to the client, and not rely on the client to create the content. Examples of this approach working well are:

- **Human resources policies.** Given the legalities involved, it is often preferred that the consultant present to the organization the parameters on what constitutes fair versus unfair practices. The client would not typically be in a position to generate the content as well as an expert in the particular field of study covered by the project. Rather than try to interpret and assess the legalities of situations on their own, clients will often ask a consultant to assist them and explain the statutes.
- **Research projects.** Depending on the kind of research being done, there might be times when the consultant has a more experienced background than the client and should provide the necessary content. For instance, if a client is considering a new market, but does not know the specifics of how to do business in that marketplace, or if a client is unsure of whether a particular acquisition target is properly valued, the consultant can guide the process and also ensure that the right metrics or criteria are applied to the decision making.

There is an old joke that applies here that might be worth sharing. A customer is exasperated by a washing machine that does not operate correctly and calls in a repair person to fix it. What follows is their dialogue upon the repair person entering the person's home:

Customer: This washing machine is very temperamental and only works some of the time. I've read the troubleshooting instructions three times and can't seem to find out what the trouble is with the machine.

Repair Person: (looking over the machine and not saying a word, but nodding and adding "uh-huh" as the customer speaks)

Customer: What do you think the problem is?

Repair Person: This oughta' do it! (moves right hand over the front of the machine in circular motion before stopping and then forcefully shoving the machine so that it rocks back slightly and upon landing immediately starts whirring and working)

Customer: Wow that is a relief! Thanks.

Repair Person: That will be $150. I accept cash or checks, no credit cards.

Customer: $150! For pushing the machine? How do you figure that is a fair price?

Repair Person: It is only $5 to push the machine. It is $100 to know that it needed to be pushed and another $45 to know where to push it!

What the client sees might be the result of years of experience and wisdom built up over many projects. While it might appear simple or not hard work to the uninitiated, it is the result (in this case, a working washing machine) of the consultant's knowing what to do, when to do it, and how to do it that is truly being paid for, and not the actual action.

Although the client is paying for the consultant's expertise, there have been times in my own experience when I suggest that the client provide me with examples of reports, data, previous results of actions taken with customers, etc., and weave them into exercises or use them as case studies to make specific points within the workshop. Even in those instances where I might choose to change the names of the accounts or the time frames referred to in an effort to create a generic example for training purposes, the client still has to contribute to the project's content. While it is not an effort to slide out of doing work or to collect a fee without doing anything for it on my part, the client will often be in possession of information or content that I can apply as part of the project's objectives to successfully complete the skill development of participants.

Communication

Another point of potential strife in managing consultants and specifically in the aligning of expectations between client and consultant is the process to be used for communicating between and among the parties involved on the project. The communication issue is one that appears over and over throughout all consultant and client relationships, and it can prove particularly vexing in the management of the relationship.

The first communication issue to be resolved is the communication from the consultant to the client. Given the complexity, multi-phased nature, and pace of many projects, the decision must be reached as to who within the consulting firm will speak for the project in its entirety. Due to the specialized tasks to be done on a component or within a particular stage of the entire project, it is not at all uncommon for consultants to be assigned to certain aspects of the project based on their expertise. However, the project needs to be managed in total by someone who is recognized as speaking for the consulting organization in its entirety. This consultant is authorized to commit resources for the consulting firm, address issues with the client, and communicate status, progress, and barriers or obstacles preventing success for the project in its entirety.

It is rather difficult to reach consensus on appropriate next steps without this person within the consulting organization. Owing to the somewhat narrow focus of some of the experts (who only see the project in terms of their own specialization area, and not the greater picture), the chaos that would occur would be insurmountable if there wasn't someone with a broader perspective tasked with managing the project and communicating back to the client.

On the client side, the same risks exist. The client cannot have multiple people charged with managing the project in its entirety. While components of the project might be best managed by subject-matter experts in that area within the client company, it is not going to be a successful project if multiple people feel empowered to direct the efforts of the consultant for the entire project. Just as the consultant needs to ultimately speak with one voice to the client, the client needs to provide a single point person as well for communicating with the consultant on issues that pertain to the global nature of the project.

None of the above removes the value of assigning a team of employees to work with a consultant to address a particular initiative, but for decisions that impact the total project, it is still necessary to have one vote that has more sway than all the others or projects can get hopelessly mired in deadlocks and political in-fighting that never allow the project to proceed successfully.

Once the people have been assigned to address the project communication between the client and consulting organization, it is necessary to determine what exactly is to be communicated and what constitutes appropriate communication.

For some projects and project leaders, there are formal weekly status reports that are to be written and submitted on a very regular basis and according to a very rigid format. In many of my own contracts, I offer that option as a way to assure the client that they will not be surprised by anything I uncover from surveys or interviews on longer-term projects. As a consultant, I feel it is my obligation to keep my client contact in the know as I collect data. While I might protect confidences of individuals and ensure that people can speak freely with me without fear of repercussion, I also do not want to spring a shocking discovery on my client contact and catch that person unaware of what I have found. Invariably, the client will prefer that I *not* submit weekly reports. It is as if my willingness to do so ensures them that they will be kept apprised and therefore they are not inclined to want to have to read through anything that is not absolutely essential.

More times than not, the client will just request that I let them know what progress I am making and if there are roadblocks that need to be addressed and removed so that I can continue to make sufficient progress on the project. In exchange for that, I am to let them know if there is something I have uncovered that would qualify as a "shocking" finding.

Other clients, though not sticklers for the detailed formal report, are very comfortable with an occasional e-mail or phone conversation to update them on the project's progress. Just as a precaution, I would suggest that both client and consultant treat these communiqués as formal documents and save them in the same way that they would a more detailed report. Just in the event that there is a misunderstanding at some point down the road, the e-mails can be reviewed to ensure that information was communicated. What I also recommend is that even voice mail messages be summarized and put into writing (doing so via e-mail is okay most of the time). Seeing one's understanding in writing or having the understanding of the voice mail you just left for the other person played back to you in writing can often identify misunderstandings early on and allow them to be addressed immediately.

With the advent of e-mails, there are some inherent risks that need to be addressed:

- Using a cc: or copying others on a message that is meant for only one person's eyes can be embarrassing or worse. Be careful when replying: Be sure you reply only to the person(s) you wish to see the message and don't just click "reply all" when you do not intend for that message to be widely broadcast.
- E-mails are permanent. Once sent, an e-mail can be printed and distributed to others, and you have lost control of how the message will be passed around, how the message will be prefaced and appended to, or how sections could be lifted and copied into other e-mail messages and attributed to you. Be very careful what is sent in an e-mail and make sure it is not something that is better discussed in person.
- While an e-mail is a relatively informal form of communication, it is also something that will be judged for accuracy and used to discern future direction on projects. Humor, irony, gestures, and tone do not translate well on e-mails. Be certain that you are very clear in your e-mail communications.

As a client, you want to be sure that consultants assigned to your project understand the confidential nature of the work to be done. Ordinarily, you would expect the consulting organization management to ensure that that message is well understood by the organization's members. It can't hurt, though, to meet and remind the consulting team of the requirement and even require that everyone on the project submit a signed non-disclosure or confidentiality form if the project is especially sensitive. As such, the consulting organization should be made aware that hallway and hotel lobby discussions about the project are prohibited, and other public areas are off limits for discussion of the project. While it is not typically essential that this kind of secrecy be maintained, if the project is one that demands this level of security, elevators and public phones are not places where project work should be mentioned.

Within the client, it is also highly recommended that references to work being done by a particular consultant also only occur between those with an absolute need-to-know basis. Again, as most projects do not require this level of restricted communication, it will be rare when it needs to be enforced, but in those instances where it is needed, care must be taken. Cafeterias, car pool shuttles, and even lavatories are not places where projects should be discussed if there is the potential for people to overhear and either misinterpret or use the information for their own purposes (often contrary to the stated mission of the project as it happens).

One of the ways to ensure there is sufficient and timely communication is to create mileposts within the project where status reports/updates/decisions on whether to proceed occur. As mentioned in the contracting chapter, building in strategic points of the project's evolution for review and ensuring sufficient progress and the appropriateness of the project's completion are highly recommended. In the event of a highly controversial project, there are occasions where the mileposts provide an opportunity for the client to determine that it no longer makes strategic sense to pursue the project based on new information uncovered since the commencement of the project, and to disband the project team. In the event of a change in priorities as a result of market conditions or other factors, it might provide the consultant and the client a chance to react to the new conditions and assess the best way to address it.

When used correctly, the mileposts provide opportunity for the consultant and the client to confirm the ongoing value of the project, address issues in the project process, or progress toward completion before these issues overwhelm the project or become too large to address, thereby impacting the success of the project.

You must decide whether to schedule the meetings around these project mileposts for off-site locations or at either the consultant's site or the client's offices based on the material to be covered in the meeting (if it even requires a face-to-face meeting). If the meeting is likely to be long and require a great deal of focus, an off-site location would probably be more suitable. Holding an intense meeting when the client or consultant is in their office is difficult since others can too easily stop by, call, or try to contact them during the meeting. On the other hand, if the meeting is likely to require the input of many people for short durations of time, it might be advantageous to conduct the meeting in the office so that those people can participate for their section of the meeting, then return to their other responsibilities. It also permits more scheduling flexibility: In case something runs longer or shorter than anticipated, the next person can more easily accommodate the change in schedule if they're at their office and allowed to work on other projects or assignments in the interim.

Providing Feedback

In the course of a project, there will be occasions or times when it is necessary to provide feedback to the consultant on the project or some aspect of the way the project is being managed or handled. The first obstacle to be overcome is the one that was mentioned previously in this chapter—the fear that the consultant is above having to respond to client feedback or even that the client does not have a right to provide feedback. It might be helpful to remember that the job title is not "Deity" but "Consultant," and the role of the consultant is to provide assistance to the executive or client. Therefore, it is not only acceptable that feedback be provided, it is essential for the success of the project.

Having established that, it is also good business practice to provide constructive, not destructive, feedback. I am not overly concerned about the feelings or ego of the consultant in this instance; the consultant can assuage his or her bruised self-confidence on their own time. But the project deserves input and insight that draws the effort closer to success and not being held hostage in a battle of nonproductive criticisms flying back and forth between client and consultant.

To accomplish this, the feedback must be direct and specific. Instead of pointing out an issue with a complaint, "You are always late," it is preferable to say, "The success of the project demands that we accomplish things according to the agreed-upon and established schedule. When you were not able to arrive for the interviews on two successive days until 10:00 a.m. when they were scheduled for 9:00 a.m., it set the project back and prevented us from moving ahead. What can be done to ensure that this does not happen again?"

Obviously, the discussion that follows will determine the success of the feedback, but the conversation is now one of problem solving and not of defensive posturing.

On a more positive side, sharing with the consultant that things are progressing and that you are pleased with the project to date is also highly recommended. The consultant needs to hear from you, the client, whether or not you are pleased with the project. The consultant's primary focus is on ensuring that you perceive value in the work being done, and secondarily, the consultant wants to ensure that you either are willing to be a potential future client or can provide access to others who might benefit from their services. Therefore, your satisfaction is of paramount importance to the consultant and within broad parameters and reason, your preferences will dictate the project's path to completion.

Receiving Feedback

There might be times when the consultant will provide you, the client, with feedback that is confidential, is difficult to hear, or otherwise taxes your normal approach to receiving information. Knowing how to receive the information is critical to the success of the project.

Given the consultant's unique position and assignment, there will be times when the consultant might be exposed to information that would not have been known to a client contact. The consultant might share with you news of a future plan that is not widely known by others within the organization. This is *not* the time to start burning the e-mail and phone lines playing "I've got a secret" with your cronies. If you are exposed to information that you would not otherwise have come across, you might want to remind the consultant that it is not universally known, and not to share it more broadly, but your actions based on the new-found information should be aboveboard and not be nefarious or inappropriate.

Still other times, the consultant might provide you with insights or information that you would rather not hear, or might even disagree with. In one instance, I was put in the difficult position of having to tell a manager that he was part of the problem of his group's faltering performance. Telling someone that the problem is staring them in the mirror is not easy, but fortunately for me, the person was professional enough to accept the information and work on correcting the issues that needed to be addressed.

It is human nature to want to be "right" and to want to have projects turn out the way we expect them to turn out. However, every once in a while, in the role of executive or manager, we might be unaware of variables that impact performance, or we might not correctly assess a situation. In those instances, the urge is overwhelming to try to "stack the deck" or control the outcome by soliciting only information that confirms our views and ignoring information or input that contradicts it or at least is in conflict with it. A good consultant will not permit that to happen. However, as a good executive and project manager, it is equally incumbent upon you to resist the urge to prevent objectivity by sabotaging the process. Most often, this can occur by selectively choosing which employees will provide input to surveys or are chosen to be included on a project. If an executive selects only those employees who have already shown a similarity in thought and actions to their own to contribute to a findings report, then the results will not surprise anyone when they mirror the executive's own thoughts.

Related to this, when I am asked to perform a needs analysis or a personnel assessment, I often ask the client to provide me with names of more than just the absolute best performers. Contrary to the intuitive belief that going to the best will provide you with the skills, knowledge areas, and approaches to be used with the other employees, the needs of the best performers and the skills of those performers might be so vastly different than the rest of the organization that unduly representing them in a survey might skew the results in a way that is not accurate or in the organization's best interests. The selection of survey or interview targets is a skill unto itself and is not one that should be taken too lightly if wide-ranging changes are to occur as a result of the survey's findings.

I have also been asked (thankfully not more than once or twice) by client contacts to re-interpret or even change the weighting I provide to certain criteria in order to prove their conclusions were right (even if confronted by evidence to the contrary). At those times, I had a decision to make. Do I follow the client's wishes at the risk of losing objectivity and credibility? Do I stand resolute and not yield on something that I hold very strong convictions about? I have made a personal choice not to be blinded by fees when it comes to purposely ignoring information or reconfiguring the evaluative criteria in order to make the data conform to my client's wishes.

As a client, trying to bend the data to fit your viewpoint will not result in anything but distrust. If I as the consultant am asked to do that, for sure the employees under this executive have been asked to do it on other projects previously. Once asked for, anything else reported after that can never be trusted as being the result of objective fact-finding. Executives who ask that of consultants do not have the support of their departments and therefore are likely ineffectual at implementation because they are not trusted.

Project Scope Creep

A major contention that consultants have with clients and the management of projects is the misperception about the depth and comprehensiveness of a project. It is for this reason that so much attention was paid to determining objectives, contracting for services in very specific terms, and ensuring that the communication flows in both directions. It is the bane of all consultants that at some point the client is going to ask (hopefully innocently), "Is it okay if you add a few more… (interviews, surveys, participants in the training executions, etc.)?" Or, the request will be, "As long as you are doing 'x,' why not also do 'y'?" Another request consultants hear is, "Would you mind asking the interviewees (or analyzing) these additional questions?"

No matter what the request, the answer should be, "Yes, I do mind" (unless there is sufficient growth to the fee as well to offset the work to be done). The consultant makes his or her living by providing services for compensation. Asking the consultant (even if done innocently) to produce more work or provide deeper contribution without remuneration is not appropriate. If you want the additional work, expect to pay for it. Asking a consultant to endure a creeping project scope that gets wider and wider or deeper and deeper is tantamount to asking that person to give away free services. Any consultant who agrees to that deserves the additional work for no additional pay, and any clients that accept the additional work for no compensation deserve whatever quality of work is delivered.

As much of my business is training or skill development related, I will occasionally be asked by a client contact to join the most senior-level person in attendance over lunch during a full-day training session. Every so often, the senior executive will look across the plates of food and ask me some variation of, "So, you have worked with us for half a day. How would we rank versus other groups you train?" After thinking about the best way to respond to this request for a number of years, I have decided that a non-answer is best. I simply state, "Your group is competitive with those in its referent group." Since most people have no idea what a "referent group" is, or if they do, they assume it is a comparison against the best of their competition, I rarely get asked to explain the comment. I have also been cornered on a 15-minute break between training topics and had the demand placed before me to rank the participants in terms of skills and likelihood of success. I usually defer to the inability to provide an answer on the spot, but that I would be more than willing to send a proposal outlining how I could assist them in acquiring that knowledge. Funny thing is, I have never had a request to send the proposal to the person asking after I offer to do so.

Managing Project Team

Once a consultant has been hired to work with a client, it is often necessary to assign employees to assist the consultant in performing the necessary tasks required to complete the project. Depending on the complexity of the project, the parameters established for what the expectations and roles are for client and consultant, the urgency of the project, and the tolerances for budgeting for consulting assistance, the internal employees assigned to assist the consultant might be delegated to the project on a full-time basis or they might be relied upon only on an as-needed basis. The tasks they perform might be as simple as providing examples of work products, answering survey questions, or agreeing to review preliminary findings. In other instances, they might be requested to perform tasks on an ongoing basis side-by-side with the consultant over the course of a multiple-month assignment.

While it might seem intuitive to expect that employees would cooperate with a consultant given that the consultant was hired to perform a task that management viewed important enough to pay for above and beyond the salaries paid to internal employees, it does not always happen quite as seamlessly as that. It should come as no surprise that there are occasional issues between management and employees, consultant and employees, and consultant and management in the execution of the project.

Obviously, when employees are part of the process and cooperate with the consultant to accomplish the task, it tends to be much more successful and is typically completed within the allotted time expected. In addition, the impact of the project can be sustained for the long-term because there is support for it from the internal employees who participated in the creation of the project's output and have a sense of ownership and commitment to it.

In order to facilitate that outcome, there are certain steps that should be taken to ensure a productive working relationship between consultant, employees assigned to the project, and management:

1. Offer internal employees explanations about why the consultant is being used.
2. Explain what the project is designed to provide or what is at stake (success will provide us with "x," and failure will result in "y").
3. Outline what steps will be taken to accomplish the task.
4. Communicate what roles individual employees will have in supporting that outcome.
5. Determine if work ordinarily handled by the members of the project team needs to be transferred to other employees. Explain the necessity of doing so to the employees being asked to accommodate the work that was previously done by the employees newly assigned to the project team.

While the project benefits most by ensuring there is cooperation between project team members and the consultant, that should not be interpreted to mean that the project team is expected to essentially "rubber stamp" everything the consultant says or does and shy away from healthy discussions, debate, or challenging of process, findings, etc. The project team members will have ideally been selected because they have subject-matter expertise that impacts the successful completion of the project. Therefore, the project team must feel as if they are fully invested in the process and outcome, and not merely filling time or following orders.

Unfortunately, there are plenty of examples where the above does not occur. Owing to the political and highly charged nature of corporate life in many client organizations, it is not at all uncommon or unheard of for project team members to attempt to use the project assignment to further their own personal agendas, biases, or assumptions—even at the expense of delaying or hampering the success of the project.

- Some employees will resent that a consultant has been contracted for at all ("We could do that work internally. Why do we need an outsider?").
- Some employees will view their participation on the project team as an opportunity to further their own career and will seek opportunities to either "save" the project from ultimate doom, prove their point of view is superior to either those of other team members or the consultant, or ensure that the mistakes of others are widely broadcast or known in an effort to "prove" that they are better than a mistake-prone colleague.
- Other employees will refrain from keeping certain information confidential, will release information earlier than agreed upon in order to demonstrate how well connected they are, or will use "secrets" for their own advantage.
- Certain employees might view the consultant as the competition and will do what they can to injure the consultant's chances for success on the project.

In one situation, I was called upon by a client to develop what was referred to as "user acceptance training" for a group of employees who were to test a new software application before it was more widely rolled out to the organization. The premise was to train these employees on how to use the application, and then permit them to trial it on their jobs and respond back with what other improvements would need to be made to the software for it to be an even easier tool or resource for completing job tasks. In building the training, it was necessary that I have copies of the software so that I could develop the course content. One of the project team members did everything he could to ensure that I was not handed updates to the software in a timely fashion so that my training was referring to screens or fields that had been changed in a revision to the application and would clearly confuse trainees who would be unable to follow the training flow or logic. In addition, he challenged me on my software programming ability (the project I was assigned was to train, not to develop the application) and was openly belligerent to any suggestions I had for improving the software. I ultimately was relieved of the assignment by the client because of too many complaints about the lack of progress and the poor climate of the project team. Imagine my surprise when I found out that I was replaced by another consulting organization who assigned a junior consultant to that project who just so happened to be the wife of the difficult project team member!

Non-Project Team Communication

As important as it is to communicate with the members of the project team about the day-to-day, ongoing tasks and assignments, there is also the need to communicate with other members of the organization who have indirect or supportive contributions to make to the success of the project. When projects are multi-phased and the fee payment is to occur on a staggered basis throughout the duration of the project, it is recommended that the corporate accounts payable people be introduced to the consultant and that they at least exchange contact numbers so that they can follow up with one another on issues of payment, invoice tracking, etc. In companies where it is preferred that the executive have all contact and follow up with the internal function of accounts payable on behalf of their chosen vendors, then I would advise the executive to alert accounts payable to the project's existence and explain what the project will consist of in terms of length of contract, number of anticipated invoices, any agreements struck about payment terms (timing, authorizations, etc.), and whether the executive or someone she or he designates from within the company will be the primary contact person with accounts payable on behalf of the consultant and the project.

Communication with other executives is also important. While you might feel that the project is yours to manage and don't really want or need other executives within your organization to meddle in your project (I had one client that used to refer to it as "playing in my sandbox"), it is still advisable to provide updates to others within the organization on what the status is of the project, what progress has been made, what remains to be done, and any successes achieved to date. While this does not have to be an elaborate marketing campaign if the project does not merit or warrant that, it is good business practice to let others know at least top-line results; this will go a long way to removing the doubt, mystery, and distrust that can result from no information being shared. One way to stop rumors from forming and halt people's fears of the unknown from filling the void with misinformation is to share information and make everyone feel that the project is an open and positive initiative that benefits all.

Consultant Wish List

Left to their own devices, a consultant will take the initiative to contact as many people in the organization as possible and will seek opportunities to solicit future business with other functions, departments, or executives. While most consultants will do this in a way that is nonobjectionable and would not reflect poorly on you or your decision to bring the consultant into the company on the assignment, it is still something you should manage and not leave to chance. Most consultants wish for a client contact who is willing to introduce other executives (preferably with budgets to spend on outside resources), "grease the skids" a bit by playing up the contribution being made, and then leave him or her to do their own selling.

You have the obligation to the organization to keep the consultant focused on the task at hand first and foremost. Any solicitation of business should be done in a way that does not interfere with either the project or other organizational business. While the consultant might have future sales needs to meet, that is not your overriding concern when working with the consultant.

When I worked for a time in a corporate assignment as a full-time employee, I worked with a consultant who charged me with being the eyes and ears for her next assignment. She claimed that she had the authorization of my manager's manager to do so (which made me wonder if there was a side deal struck where the executive was to receive some "kickback" for all business done with the consultant). I never challenged her and I did not question my manager about it, but I definitely did not perform well on that task. Her need to solicit future employment was not something I viewed as essential for me, my career, or my organization's well-being.

Friend or Not?

One of the aims of salespeople (and consultants are salespeople) is to develop rapport with their prospect or client. The business of selling consulting services is highly dependent on the strength of the relationship, and therefore, the consultant seeks to befriend the prospect as quickly and as thoroughly as possible.

Very often, the consultant has a rather charismatic way and is a dynamic and engaging speaker who draws people to him or her. Regaling people with stories of past client projects (hopefully with the names changed to protect the confidentiality of the client and the project), travel experiences, and humorous occurrences while working is often second nature for the consultant. Many client contacts want to live vicariously through the consultant and enjoy the stories and the adventures of the consultant. What might not be evident at first blush though is that this plays well into the consultant's desire to be viewed as a "friend" and not as a provider/vendor/supplier of services.

Human nature being what it is, once the relationship has a platonic component to it, it is rather difficult for a client to "fire" or "dismiss" someone they have come to view as a friend. The psychological implications become more pronounced when you have to tell a friend bad news than when you have to relay bad news to someone you consider merely an acquaintance or associate. Smart consultants will ingratiate themselves as quickly and as deeply as they can in an effort to thwart off any early attempts to sever the relationship before it has had a chance to blossom. In the final analysis, much of what is being sold in a consulting project is the "trust" that has been established. The "product" being purchased is more often a promise of a result, and not an actual physical entity that the client can hold and evaluate. It requires the client to visualize an outcome that has yet to happen and is only likely to happen as a result of a series of steps that the client is unsure will produce the desired result. Therefore, the importance of being viewed as a friend is critical for the consultant: A friend would not steer you wrong. A friend is someone you trust. The dynamic changes from being viewed as someone who is peddling or selling something, to someone who is an advocate for you and wants what is best for you.

Many buyers working for major retail chains (Safeway, Wal-Mart, etc.) are rotated out of their assignments and are given a new product line to purchase in an effort to keep the relationships with salespeople from forming too deeply. Rather than allow a particular salesperson to become too friendly and thereby leverage that friendship into more favorable opportunities for the salesperson's company (at the expense of the retailer), the buyers are in the position for only 24 months or less and are changed out before a relationship can solidify too strongly.

Gifts

The topic of gift giving is one that often causes polarity of opinions and divergence amongst both consultants and clients. The premise of the gift giving from the consultant's perspective is to thank someone for their business and acknowledge their trust/faith/willingness to do business with the consultant. On the surface, that seems like a smart business decision and a well-mannered action to take.

The downside to this practice is that it opens up the opportunity to "buy" the business from the client in exchange for ever increasingly expensive gifts. While a gift of a bottle of imported wine is not likely to sway a hundred thousand dollar project to one consultant over another, opportunities to travel, tickets to hard-to-get events, hotel stays, or all-expenses-paid time at corporate villas or chateaus might turn a few corporate heads in a favorable direction toward one consultant over another. The desire to curry favor with clients by means that are aboveboard, gray, and even inappropriate (or illegal) will not cease, but the ethics and standards followed by clients in not yielding to these practices can begin to cast them in a less-positive light. Through further education and corporate controls, anyone who succumbs to these efforts will be viewed less positively and, in some instances, will lose their job.

Many companies have cracked down on this practice by forbidding employees to receive gifts at all, or any gifts above a certain amount (try giving a car as a gift to someone as 1,000 separate packages, each containing value of less than $50). Now, some client contacts have gotten around this by having the salesperson send a gift to the home and addressed to the spouse so that it is not "technically" sent to the executive. Obviously, that is an inappropriate action and one that is not likely to be looked upon favorably by anyone who discovers the charade.

In my own business, I have taken clients out to dinner or sent golf shirts or other attire with a corporate logo, calculators, pens, and other corporate gifts to clients to thank them for their business. But I take a very hard stance not to cross the line into illegal activities or offering a bribe to conduct business with me. My integrity and credibility is too important to me, and any consultant who does try to buy the business from a client through excessive gift giving ought to be viewed critically and cynically by the client. As enticing as the gifts might be, what the client must decide is the real value of the consultant's efforts on the project.

I will also share one story that was told to me by a trainer I had the good fortune of hearing facilitate a sales-training session. Mike Bosworth told a story of a salesperson who was competing for a client's business with a company that had a high-profile athlete affiliated with them. When a client was nearly ready to sign a large deal with this competitor, the competitor's management would often trot out the celebrity athlete for a "meet and greet" golf outing or a photo opportunity with the prospect's management. The hope was that the client would be so awed by the athlete and the company that provided the experience, that it would "seal the deal" for them.

This salesperson, knowing that he was running neck and neck with the competitor, used the athlete against them by telling the prospect that he knew that it was a close call, but he did not want the prospect to be unduly swayed by things outside the appropriate decision criteria for this project. He further elaborated that when the other company presents their final offer and brings the athlete to see them, takes them for a ride in the corporate jet, and puts them on the best golf courses for free—as they do for all their best prospects—it was his hope that the prospect could see through the hype.

What the salesperson knew, and the prospect did not, is that the athlete was only used for sales over a threshold, and this project was below that. The competitor did not fly the prospect anywhere, did not offer free golf, and did not introduce the prospect to the athlete. The message received by the prospect was that "Your business is not important to us." The prospect was insulted that his project was not seen as being worthy of attention by the other company and signed the deal with the salesperson who did not have the athlete affiliation.

Working with Other Consultants

On some very large projects or complex assignments that cut across multiple functions or specialization areas, a client will occasionally hire multiple consultants and expect them to work together for the good of the project or the client's benefit. While it is possible that this does happen, I have never participated in a project that ended successfully where the client brought multiple consultants together who had not approached the client cooperatively. More often, what happens is a tug-o-war between or among the consultants as to which one is the "alpha dog" of the consultants. Much time is wasted and energy is expended trying to muscle in on the other consultant's portion of the assignment than is really productive.

Consultants are, as a rule, highly competitive people who have high self-opinions and possess very large egos. While in many instances that helps fuel their ability and desire to perform in a role that demands high energy and the ability to multi-task and accomplish much on tight time frames and with little direction, it can also turn very ugly when those skills are pitted against others.

If you as a client have determined that it is necessary to segment projects out to different consultants who did not bid on the total project together, it would be to your best advantage to call a meeting with all consulting organizations involved and be *very* specific as to what you expect, to what your objectives are, and to let it be known that you are managing the project. If you decide to let one of the consultants manage other consultants, you have just written an invitation for warfare in your very own hallways.

Far more productive and much more likely to be better managed is an approach where you scope the entire project and offer it to larger consulting firms with the provisions that they are to sub-contract with specialists of your choosing. In this way, you ensure you are getting the best of all worlds: the benefits of the large-scale consultants and the niche focus of the smaller players, without the sniping and internecine fighting. The two organizations need each other to work cooperatively, or they both stand to lose. In this situation, you can also go to the consultant you contracted with overall and register any complaints, changes of scope, etc., and not have to negotiate with two organizations. Your commitment is to the one consulting group, and their commitment is to the other consulting group based on the project's parameters.

As long as we are talking about subcontracting consulting work, it is rather common for a larger organization (or even smaller ones) to contract with a client for work that might be beyond their current capabilities, or may be within their skill set, but at the time of the project, their expert resources are otherwise engaged on other projects. In these instances, it is often resolved by the consulting organization subcontracting with a niche specialist consulting organization to perform very narrowly defined roles on the project. Often, these consultants are introduced to you as belonging to the consulting organization you hired and you believe they are employees. In some instances, they are subcontractors that the consulting organization has selected to use for the project. While that might be an irrelevancy to you in many instances, it is wise to be aware of that likelihood if that is something that would change how you feel about the consulting organization's fitness to complete the project or would impact your decision to use that particular consultant.

Consulting organizations that are hired on as "transparent" subcontractors (that is, the client is unaware that they are not truly members of the contracting organization) will occasionally get aggressive and try to cut side deals with the client to remove the "middleman" from the agreement and offer to complete the work for a lesser fee than the contracting firm. While clearly not something that the contracting consulting firm would ever want to encourage or see done, it is also something that you as a client should not look fondly upon. The ethics in doing that are so low that it should raise questions about what other business practices this organization uses and whether they can be trusted with your confidential information. A consultant who would sell a project out from the contracting consulting firm would equally be suspect of using your proprietary information with another client or as discussion fodder with your competitor. Avoid these charlatans if they approach you; they are the scourge of the consulting business.

Checklist for Managing Consultants

1. Have you clearly spelled out and communicated the skills and level of experience you expect the consultant to provide? Have you specified the accommodations you are willing to provide? Are you and the consultant aligned on what roles each of you will play in the completion of the project?
2. Is there a communication protocol in place (weekly or bi-weekly status meetings, e-mail updates, etc.)?
3. Are there mileposts established where you will confirm/reconfirm the status of the project based on any new information, corporate direction, or other factors germane to the completion of the project?
4. Has a process been developed for sharing feedback between the consultant and yourself?
5. Is there an understanding with the consultant of what is confidential, what is to be shared, and what is for "those with a need to know only"?
6. Is the scope of the project sufficiently spelled out to accomplish the intended objectives? Is there a need to re-address the depth of the project's parameters *before* asking for additional work as part of the existing project?
7. Has the project team been selected? Have they been communicated to so that they understand their role and what is expected of them in the completion of the project?
8. Has the consultant been told what is permissible and what is not with regard to soliciting additional business during the project?
9. Have you selected multiple consultants to work on more than one aspect of the project? Have you determined how you will ensure that there are sufficient controls in place to keep them focused on the project and not on unseating each other?

Working with Consultants

Key Learning Points:

- Identifying the executional steps necessary to complete the project
- Avoiding the urge to broaden project scope
- Reinforcing the importance of providing feedback throughout the project to those who are contributing/stand to be impacted by the project
- Communicating with the consultant on project matters only
- Importance of regular communication
- Addressing conflict positively
- Methods for sustaining interest in the project
- Project life cycles

The keynote of progress, we should remember, is not merely doing away with what is bad; it is replacing the best with something better.

— Edward A. Filene

You might have noticed that throughout this book to this point, I have emphasized the "make ready" steps in what might be perceived as rather minute detail. While this might have appeared to be overkill in a sense, its importance will become clear during this chapter. In this chapter, the focus will be on the steps to take once the project has commenced and how to maximize the results from the efforts of the consultant and any internal members of your organization assigned to the project.

If the preparatory work elucidated in the first five chapters of this book has been done correctly and thoroughly, this step becomes little more than the second clause in the bromide, "plan the work, work the plan." While not necessarily easy to do, it is conceptually simple (you know *what* needs to be done, but *how* to do it is not always apparent). The hardest part is avoiding some of the pitfalls that can befall well-intentioned clients and consultants that allow other extraneous issues to creep into the work on the project and distract or taint the process from its main thrust.

Stick to the Project

In my experience, after all the work has been completed to determine objectives, decide on an appropriate scope, create a project plan, assign internal employees to the project (if needed), and identify target goals and evaluative criteria to use to measure success, the most common cause of projects that do not ultimately deliver the expected results is failure to follow the agreed-upon project parameters.

The concept of "scope creep" was introduced previously as if it were an insidious fungus that covers a project until it ultimately creates a wholly different project than the one originally being pursued. As attractive as it might seem in the interest of efficiencies, it rarely is a good idea to try to do more than is planned for when conducting consulting assignments. Upon occasion, I will be asked to conduct a day and a half workshop in a regional or divisional office for a client, and then as the project draws near, other people within the client will realize that having the attendees all in the same location for a period of time is too good of an opportunity to pass up. They decide to "append" other training or presentations onto the scheduled training session, turning an eight-hour day of training followed by another six-hour day of training into three full days of training/presentation/ show and tell/etc.

Invariably, the comments received back from attendees (solicited on feedback forms, or if not provided with that opportunity, spontaneously provided as if the opinion is a combustible accelerant that must be expectorated for fear of self-immolation) are some variation of:

- "Too much information for us to digest in one session."
- "Would have been better if it could have been broken up over multiple meetings."
- "I am so confused, data overload!"

As a result of the decision to try to stuff too much information into too few hours, and ignoring the original consulting plan, neither objective is met (not the original one that had to share focus, time, and attention with the later addition, nor the "last minute, as long as we have you all here today, this will only take a few minutes/hours/etc., and it really is important" topic). Frustrated, the attendees are unsure of what to focus on first, how to prioritize, and what is expected of them. The presenters of the add-on topics, suffering from topic myopia, only see the impact on their little piece of the puzzle and scratch their heads when the attendees do not seem to react and change behaviors. The consultant is held accountable for the original training not being as successful as anticipated, and the client contact is left to wonder if the attendees are incapable of learning, the consultant is a charlatan, and the other presenters are clueless about the pressures faced by the rest of the organization.

The harsh reality is that all this would have been avoidable had the original plan been well thought out, approved by all affected parties, and then followed as agreed upon. However, it has been my unfortunate position as a consultant to see client contacts become overwhelmed by requests by others within the organization to "carve out" some time from the planned program for their own needs. Rarely is that successful.

The other death knell for consulting projects is asking for insight, input, or participation in a process (for example, brainstorming with selected individuals, surveying team members, or interviewing job incumbents) and then not delivering on your commitment or promised result (that is, a better process, a more equitable compensation plan, enhanced resources or tools to conduct the work, a formal succession plan, or any other consulting project outcome).

Employees or customers and suppliers who are asked to contribute to a consulting project often do so out of a sense of commitment to the requesting party. They might be leery of how the results will be used, so there is a demand that the objectives of the project be explained up front. In addition, they might want to know if their input will be attributable back to the them; if it is not attributable and there is no retribution possible for those who are asked for input, then employees are likely to provide much different insights than if their input is attributable. Employees will also want to know who will have access to their input and to be informed about what will be done with their input.

Asking people for their perspective on something raises their level of expectations that someone cares, is aware of the issues, and has a desire to improve the situation. While not everyone's suggestion is feasible, and not all input is necessarily a call to action, the minimum a consulting project that has asked for the contribution of others owes to the participants (and more broadly the organization) is an explanation of the findings, an implementation plan, and rationale for how the plan makes good business sense in light of the contributions sought. Tell people what was shared with the consultant (in aggregate so that no one is identified where possible and appropriate), what steps are being taken to resolve a known problem or address a particular issue that caused the need for the consulting project, and what further contributions will be expected/needed in execution or implementation. Finally, it would also be helpful to share what the achievement of the goal will mean to the individuals (savings of "x" dollars corporately, more efficient hiring procedures, less downtime on computer systems, etc.).

"Consultant" Is *Not* Another Word for Clergy

Given the nature of some assignments and some working relationships between client and consultant, it is more the rule than the exception that there will be many hours of working side-by-side cooperatively and more than a few long hours devoted to the project at odd times (evenings, weekends, early mornings, etc.). With this kind of working environment, it is rather easy to build rapport and trust with the consultant when you are both working for the success of a common project. Every now and again, however, this relationship takes on an odd twist. The consultant is seen as someone who is "safe" to talk to about matters that might be outside the boundaries of the project. The consultant is sometimes perceived as not only being somewhat of an "expert" in the area hired for, but in other areas as well. The consultant is not a competitive threat as far as promotions or more favorable assignments within the company, therefore the executive doesn't have to worry about repercussions if admissions of weakness or doubt are made to the consultant. The consultant is assumed to be neutral and objective, and therefore, non-judgmental.

Many consultants have come to view their client contacts as friends (remember the earlier reference to consultants striving to do this as a matter of self-preservation), and to a certain extent, that is natural. Clients that hire consultants are likely to share the same views on things, at least to the extent that it impacts the project and likely beyond that as well. A bonding of sorts is often inevitable when two ambitious, intelligent, and progressive thinkers align themselves (and by their own definition, if they each choose the same project, seek the same outcome, and agree to work together, then they must be ambitious, intelligent, and progressive).

However, the client that decides to use the consultant as a "Father Confessor" and share all the dirt about the company or other employees within the company—or their own personal issues about family, marriage, and career choices—is putting the consultant in an untenable position. The consultant is (in most instances) not a therapist and is not qualified to assist the executive through the issues. The consultant might have divided loyalties or allegiances within the company (he or she might have access to or work with others), and the shared information might cause conflict within the consultant as to which relationship should supercede the other. Ethics aside for the moment, the reality is that when confronted with this situation, you are allowing the consultant to make a decision as to what to share or if to share, and by all rights, this should be your decision.

The safest approach is to be friendly, cordial, and professional with the consultant and restrict matters to project-related conversation or other polite conversation that you would not mind hearing shared with others within the company or industry. Unless you have contracted specifically with the consultant to provide this kind of guidance or direction, discussions of personal worth, foibles of other personnel, and your grand schemes to start your own business to compete with your current employer should be reserved for family gatherings or other places where it is not likely to ever surface and shame you in front of peers or supervisors.

When I was just starting out in consulting, I worked with a woman who was tasked with being my client contact on the project, but was not the person with the signatory authority to approve my expenses. This person proceeded to tell me on one long multiple-city trip about how she had tried to get pregnant and failed numerous times (which I expressed the suitable amount of sympathy for given that I really did not know her well at all and was taken aback that she would share this), how she has been having an affair with the signatory (now, what do I do with *that* information? Congratulate her? Nod and ask for more salacious details?), and how she would be leaving the company with him shortly to start a business (is that a clue to me that I had better get all of my expense reports in before they leave if I expect to get paid?). I was frozen as to how to respond, so I said nothing besides, "uhhh – huh-hhh." I figured that can't be the wrong thing to say, if it wasn't exactly the right thing. An even better solution would have been to have not had to reply in any way because the client had the good sense not to raise issues that were really none of my concern, did not directly impact that particular project, and placed me in a position of having to know information that was obviously inappropriate for me to have known.

Sharing Thoughts

Now, that is not to say that the consultant should not be told or communicated with on those matters that are directly relevant to the project. If, as a client, you are unsure of whether something is appropriate to share, I would advise you to share it and let the consultant sort it out. It is better to over-communicate and share more than necessary, than to hold information back that could have had a direct impact on the project.

In matters related to communication and sharing of ideas, observations, status of project, etc., it is recommended that the flow and exchange of ideas be as free as possible between client contact and consultant. As a strong proponent of communicating and remaining in close contact with my client, I suggest scheduled status updates (even if at minimum they are the go/no-go steps), but if something should arise in between those scheduled communication sessions, I endorse sharing the new found information and deciding on appropriate courses of action to be taken. In many instances, the answer might be to address it at the go/no-go steps, but failing to at least surface the issues at the earliest point of awareness is a strategy for which I can see no positive outcome.

Waiting to be solicited for input or holding on to vital information because no one directly asked you for it is tantamount to torpedoing the project through inactions. The protocol and convention in communicating with the consultant should not interfere with the free flow of information that is essential, but the information should come from one person within the client organization. It is unfair to ask the consultant to respond to multiple points of view and recommended approaches from within the organization. Therefore, there should be a communication loop within the client to ensure that information is shared both "vertically" (from subordinate to boss) and "horizontally" (between and among different functions of the company). The same communication process should be in place on the consultant side as well; communication should be directed in a way that the primary consultant with client contact responsibility is aware of issues and can speak knowledgeably about them with the client.

The corollary to this is the obvious matter of also providing information that is requested. While it is appropriate to share project-relevant matters as they arise before being asked, the more obvious expectation is that when asked for information that has a direct bearing on the project, that you share perspectives, history, status, etc., of the matter being asked about.

When forming project teams, assign internal employees who will be responsible for responding to the requests that the consultant might have directly related to their work on the project. Being stymied from making progress because no one assumes the responsibility for ensuring that requests are responded to is frustrating for both consultant and for other project team members and can easily lead to a less-than-optimum project outcome.

The dynamic of the consultant making a request to an employee can sometimes lead to resentment or a lessening of the request's priority. I have worked with clients that anticipate this response and intercept it in one of two ways. Some clients require that all informational requests come through the senior member of the project team and then be doled out to the appropriate resource internally, only this time with the authority of the senior member behind the request. Other clients have the senior member of the team emphasize in either a meeting with team members or in a written correspondence to team members that they are to treat the consultant's requests for information or assistance as if they were coming from the senior executive. The "unsaid" message is that any team members wavering from that effort would be accountable to the senior executive and had better have a rather defensible reason or there would/could be repercussions.

Communication Fundamentals

The process of communicating between consultant and client adheres to the same protocols as any other business communication between people working on projects that at times involve sensitive or proprietary information. Loud hallway conversations, elevator discussions, or other public discourse where eavesdroppers might misinterpret what they hear are obviously to be avoided. That is not to say that all communication is to be shrouded in secrecy and cloaked in mystery. Quite the contrary, it is beneficial to communicate with other employees not directly involved in the project as much and as often as makes sense given the parameters of the project.

As mentioned previously, the process of communication should be considered as the project is being formed. When most people think of consultant and client communication, they might be inclined to consider the more formal kind of communication usually reserved for findings reports or other key opportunities for the client and consultant to communicate. In these instances, some of the core determinants are deciding on:

- Who "speaks" for the consultant's position if there is more than one individual working on the project from the consulting firm?

- Who "speaks" for the client and is empowered to make decisions?
- What constitutes official communication?
  - Will there be reports or status meetings?
  - Do certain people have to be in attendance or in receipt of a report for it to become an official communication?
  - Is there a format to be followed?
- How often will official communication occur?
  - Who has the right to "call" for official communication?
  - Does it have to be scheduled, or can it be "ad hoc"?

In the ebb and flow of project work on a day-to-day basis, the more common form of communication is the informal communication associated with project tasks or assignments. The decisions to be made in this regard that impact the project are:

- Should the consultant be provided with a corporate e-mail address for ease of forwarding and distributing messages within the project team?
- Should all project-related requests be made in writing, or can verbal conversations suffice?
- Is any consultant assigned to the project permitted to communicate with anyone within the client, or is there a specific communication chain that is to be followed to limit the exposure of executives to consultants?

These are just some of the criteria that I have seen implemented with clients to ensure that there is a common understanding on the management of communication. Depending on the project, there might be other criteria that are relevant and deserve consideration.

Before we leave the topic of client/consultant communication, there are two other points that should be addressed. The first is the need to protect members of the project team from feeling threatened for holding unpopular or controversial ideas that might actually be in the best interests of the project. For projects to succeed, there are times when a team member might have a suggestion or an approach that potentially casts that team member in an adversarial light with either other team members or even employees not included among the team.

The need to insulate the team from repercussions as they build their solution and perhaps explore various options is critical if the team is going to feel comfortable providing their best thinking.

The other side of that coin is to expose efforts that are counter to the team's objectives and not productive to the successful completion of the project. In many instances, the client company views participation on the project team as a "perk" or recognition of one's past contribution and efforts. The project team cannot be permitted to splinter due to one person's efforts to steer the team in a direction that is contrary to the organization's needs, but might serve the personal needs of that team member.

Communication around these two issues needs to be straightforward, forthright, and unyielding. As soon as a team member feels threatened for espousing a viewpoint that is a legitimate attempt to resolve the problem confronting the team, or a member is permitted to lobby for a self-serving answer, the efforts of the team will begin to wane and will not be truly focused on generating the "best" solution, but will now be focused on providing a "satisfactory" solution to meet needs other than the best interests of the project or organization.

Stick to Objectives

During the course of projects that are longer term (typically meaning more than a couple of months in duration), it is not at all uncommon for other ideas, initiatives, or perspectives to arise that if left unchecked and not thoroughly analyzed might change the focus of the project partially or entirely. While an idea of this nature is often worthwhile and might be appropriate to pursue, if it doesn't directly impact the successful completion of the existing project or is not of such a high priority that it merits changing the direction of the existing project, it is best to treat it as a separate project or a follow-up phase. This idea should not be allowed to distract the project team, the consultant, and the other people involved on the project (interviewees, subject-matter experts called upon to assist in the completion of the project, survey respondents, etc.) from their original charge.

In working with a major manufacturer in the health and beauty care business, I had been asked to assist them with an introduction of a new software tool to users who were remotely located across the country. The original intent was to provide training and reference materials that were electronically provided (either embedded in the software application tool itself or as an adjunct CD-ROM that would be sent along with the software tool to the field offices). Along the way, one of the more ambitious members of the project team thought it would be helpful to provide a video of how to use the tool to perform the job more effectively.

When the idea was broached with the project team at headquarters, many of them were excited by the idea and quickly scurried to find the incremental budget to cover the video production expense. What no one had thought to consider were the following:

- The eventual end users of the video did not have powerful enough computers or all the components required to view and play videos on their laptops and the whole purpose was to avoid having to bring them into a central location, so sending a video to a regional office and expecting the remotely located/home-based people to view it when they came into the office was not a likely path to success.
- The users of the tool were not at all comfortable with how to load the software tool and certainly were uncomfortable with the notion of loading a separate video application onto a computer that they were not comfortable with in the first place (that was what the training was supposed to cover).
- The logistics of creating the video and then having to append it onto the original software tool proved problematic.

Now I had assumed that the primary client contact was aware of these decisions being made and had endorsed this change in objectives. But it was only when I brought the fact that we were bogged down in these issues to the attention of the primary client contact during a status meeting that I discovered he was not aware, was quite familiar with the issues that were causing the slowdown—as he himself had tried to figure out a way around it—and had called me in to request that I complete the project with the original set of objectives because it was not feasible to do it the other way.

I learned an important lesson about communicating and sticking to the objectives, and the client contact acquired a better understanding of the importance of remaining close to a project's progress, if not directly involved. The team members were correct to think in terms of the other approaches, but had not done due diligence in communicating the changes to be explored with senior management in order to get authorization and approval.

There had been a series of false starts on this project as a result, but I later learned that the project would not have been funded in its more elaborate conception because there was no budget available to authorize the new expanded scope. This provides another lesson: If there is no funding available, enlarging a project scope can happen only if the members of the project team agree to create more for less.

Handling Conflict

This past example also brings up a consideration that is likely to happen during any project: how to address conflict. It is no wonder that conflicts can occur given the environments in which many consulting projects become necessary:

- Competitive pressures
- Market conditions
- Performance declines
- Expense-saving opportunities
- Efficiency improvements

Adding to the possibility of conflict are the following personalities and working conditions that consulting projects often include:

- The "best and the brightest" from within a company assigned to assist on the project
- Tight time frames in which to produce positive results
- The perception that the project is additional work beyond the tasks ordinarily handled by project team members
- A consultant who is very self-assured and has achieved success with many clients
- An executive whose career progression or very job might be at jeopardy if the project is not successful

In some instances, conflict can be beneficial and can lead to a better solution by truly working on building and bettering each other's ideas and challenging the ideas that are less optimal. In some corporate cultures, conflict is seen as a positive and is encouraged. A perspective of healthy debate and recognition that the ideas and not the person are being challenged is the norm.

More often, conflict is seen as a detrimental byproduct of strong personalities, personal agendas, political machinations, and egos run amok. Rather than confront another, it is better to accede or acquiesce to someone else's preferences. Better to appear aligned and in agreement than to admit there is dissension or disagreement. Of course, this can also breed resentment among those impacted by the decisions that will ultimately be reached.

How conflict is handled can have huge implications for the success of the project, but one of the strong benefits of using a consultant is that the issue of conflict (at least as it relates to the use of the consultant) is often more easily handled than with internal employees. A consultant is hired for the duration of the project and at the discretion or whim of the client contact. While there are some contractual requirements regarding payment and performance criteria, once those have been met, the consultant can be separated from the project and the company is free to pursue other options.

If issues arise between the consultant and the project team, or the consultant and the client contact, it is reasonable and fair that these issues be brought to the surface and addressed to determine whether the problem is one that can be overcome, or if the problem is of such a substantial nature as to be beyond correcting. Conflicts are going to occur anytime you have the above conditions mentioned. But a conflict that is merely a difference of opinion when two people are earnestly trying to do what is best for a project (in other words, both are working toward the same goal, but have chosen different paths to get there) is a different situation than when there is conflict due to relationship issues, such as:

- Betrayal of confidences
- Distrust due to behaviors contrary to the benefit of the project/ client

- Proof of poor work or other project-related steps
- Communication breakdowns

In these situations, it might be best for a client to conclude the relationship with the consultant and strike out in a different direction with other resources (internal or another consultant) that are more in synch with the preferred methods, approaches, and working-relationship dynamics of the client.

Work from a Common Language

Under most circumstances, the consultant chosen for a project will at least be partially familiar with the client company (from having worked for them previously, from having worked with others in a similar industry, or from research the consultant might have done). This allows the consultant and the client to communicate in a lexicon of the industry and to make references to ideas and concepts known to both. A quick scan of any trade or industry-specific publication will point out the many acronyms, abbreviations, and coded ways that industry professionals communicate with each other. However, every once in a while, the jargon used by one to communicate an idea or concept might not be familiar to the other.

Early in my career when I worked as an internal employee, I worked on a project that included creating a sales training video for a new product. Being eager and ambitious (and thinking I had some creative flair), I offered to work with the vendor hired to help script, cast, shoot, and produce the video. When I got the script, there were references that I did not understand at all, but being too vain to show my ignorance, I tried to pretend I was an old pro at this. One of the references on the script that I was unfamiliar with was to a "demonstration of the product MOS." When we were shooting the video and we got to the point of the script where this reference first appeared, I demonstrated the product's use and extolled the virtues of the product in an ad lib (showing my creative flair). The director called, "CUT," and said, "David, this is M-O-S." I redid it and again added my dramatic touches to the product demonstration. The director said (this time a little less patiently), "This is without sound, M-O-S." Well, now I had to admit I was lost: "What is M-O-S?" I was then enlightened that M-O-S is a video term that is a derivation of how an old time Germanic director used to pronounce it in English "*Mit Ot Sund.*" What the director wanted was the "action" of the demonstration, but the ability to do a voice-over or apply some other scripting over the action aside from the scripted words in post-production. Often the director will use that as "safety" so that should the intended action not produce the right results, there is still opportunity to communicate the message by splicing in the action at strategic points (and if there was sound, it would identify it as having been jammed into a place that is out of sequence).

My business partner, Jeff Clow, tells a story to workshop participants that points out the need for a common language or reference equally as well. During a face-to-face meeting with an executive who Jeff was working with, the executive stressed the importance of the employees meeting a "ROAM target." Jeff, hearing this, assumed the client had established some incentive trip to Italy that was to include a visit to *Rome.* After the client used the phrase a few more times, Jeff inquired, "Just what are the components of this trip to *Rome* and how do the employees qualify?" The client looked dismissively at Jeff and asked him, "Don't you know what ROAM is?" Jeff, again, thinking it was a reference to the city, replied with his best impression of Fodor's travel guide to show he knew exactly what *Rome* is. The client then laughed and explained that ROAM is a financial term that stands for "return on assets managed." The executive wanted employees to be more efficient and productive with the assets (budgets, corporate resources, staffing, etc.) they were responsible for managing in an effort to diminish wasteful spending and nonproductive projects.

The two examples above solidify the case that making assumptions about one's understanding of terms used or concepts referenced can do the exact opposite of what they are intended to do. Rather than help clarify or provide a common reference point with which to discuss issues, these assumptions can serve to muddle and confuse. Recently, the three-letter abbreviation brigade of terms have come into common usage among business professionals, but if you are not conversant in the terms, you would be confused about what was referred to when someone used such acronyms as those listed in the table on the next page.

Commonly Used Business Abbreviations

Acronym	Term	Definition
EDI	Electronic Data Interchange	A computer-to-computer communication protocol
ECR	Efficient Consumer Response	A process that reduces inventory and more closely matches consumer demand and production
CRM	Customer Relationship Management	The aligning of all the various ways customers and suppliers interact with each other
JIT	Just In Time	A method of receiving deliveries of raw materials as needed in order to create products and ship them out with minimal "holding time"
ERP	Enterprise Resource Planning	A search for synergies across an entire company and the providing of access and sharing of information across different functions and departments where typically there were informational silos or function-specific maintenance of information that likely could be of use for others within the company

Once explained, many of these terms can be incorporated into the focus of a particular project to ensure that the output of the project is consistent with the thrust of these more large-scale projects that the client company is undertaking.

For example, when working with a client on improving their sales force's ability to reduce the number of mistakes made in sales-order processing, it is necessary for me to be able to see how my efforts support the greater ECR project that might be occurring at the same time and ensure that I am including the use of tools, processes, and approaches that are consistent with the goals of the ECR initiative. If I am unfamiliar with the term *ECR* and am not conversant in the goals and objectives of that process, I run the risk of creating a project solution that is contrary to the purpose of the larger project and might do more harm than good for my client.

Implementation Common Sense

One of the dangers in completing a project is that in the constant crisis-management approach practiced by some companies, there is a chance that the project will not pay "immediate results" or will be forgotten as more or newer priorities emerge and confront the organization. While the project might have been seen as important at one time, it is not as glamorous or contemporary as whatever has last been mentioned as an appropriate pursuit.

Upon occasion, there will be a skepticism or healthy cynicism around a consulting project that it is little more than "the flavor of the day." The skeptics believe that if left alone, it will cease to be the most important project ever undertaken and will be replaced by some other corporate-saving initiative that promises to improve employee retention, reverse stock performance, sew curtains, and fold laundry for you all at the same time! Now, there is some kernel of truth to the short attention span that some companies exhibit when it comes to changing the tried-and-true ways of doing things—always seeking the next magic bullet or secret panacea to cure all that ails them. However, there are times when the project's relevance and importance could have been sustained with some implementation guidance or forethought.

It is frustrating for both consultant and members of the project team to invest the time and energy into completing a project, truly investing themselves into doing it well, and committing their energies to producing as strong a project as possible, only to have the final report gathering dust on the shelves of the very people who can best impact its success, or have an executive presentation poorly attended because the people who need to hear the results most are unable to get to it because they are addressing the latest "firefighting exercise" and can't slow down long enough to listen and absorb the solution to the issue already addressed.

Clients can sustain the momentum of these projects long past the fanfare and enthusiasm often associated with project commencements and ensure that a project does not just wither away between the start and conclusion of the project work by:

1. Tracking compliance, performance, or other quantifiable examples of integration, progress, etc.
2. Publishing newsletters

3. Hanging wall charts/banners/posters
4. Offering incentives

Tracking. It is curious that when things are measured and shared with the people being measured, or their bosses, there is more attention paid to it than if there is no evaluation of the effort. A simple reporting of which employees have actually signed on to a system, which employees have completed a training session, or any other measurable, quantifiable evaluation of a project's use and acceptance can mean the difference between a consulting project being viewed as a success or as a failure.

Newsletters. Some clients have effectively kept the importance of a project in the minds of project "stakeholders" (those people with a stake in the success of the project, e.g., employees, customers, suppliers) by publishing and distributing newsletters that share the progress being made, highlight the achievements of the project, or in other ways communicate the status of the project as it is being completed. By reminding those impacted by the project's objective that the project is still being pursued, it reinforces the need and the company's commitment to resolving issues favorably.

Wall Charts/Banners. I have worked with clients that have piqued the interest of employees about an ongoing project by clever use of slogans, graphics, or other devices. By using clever code names for projects, engaging employees in guessing what the project is designed to do, or utilizing other "marketing" approaches to create a "buzz" around a topic, some projects have been able to sustain and even increase the level of interest in projects through banners, wall posters, announcements, etc.

Incentives. While not a new approach, providing incentives (monetary or other) for those early adapters of the new skill, process, use of the software, etc., can be quite successful in helping to reinforce the purpose of the project and assist in the implementation success.

If a project includes some "roll out" of a new approach, a cultural change, or a different process that is likely to involve resistance to it, a wise client and consultant tandem will remove some of the objections, hesitancies, or fears that the organization might have through constancy of message achieved through the above methods.

It is not reasonable to expect people to accept a new reality created by the consulting assignment (even if it makes perfect sense to do so to the project team and consultant) without challenging it and working through the psychological barriers of resistance to change. This is a time for more communication and more opportunity for employees to ask questions, not less. Some clients have made the mistake of restricting communication in an effort to reduce the errors or to carefully control the message. While those are appropriate goals, it should not come at the expense of creating a vacuum. In the face of little or no information, rumors will start, misinformation will be accepted as fact, and whole projects can be tainted before they ever had a chance to succeed.

A recent book, *The Tipping Point: How Little Things Can Make a Big Difference* (by Malcolm Gladwell, Time Warner Bookmark, 2000), emphasizes the next point to be made about gaining early acceptance of the consulting project's intent. In the book, the author explains how there are certain people within our social circles who are connectors to other people. Some are influential, and many others are connectors to influential people themselves, but are not necessarily able to directly impact things by virtue of status or responsibility. The analogy for consulting projects is to involve those people within a company who are highly regarded, have lots of informal contacts, and are able to convince others of the benefit of the project. By the sheer charisma, energy, or personal dynamism that these people have over others, they can often assist in ensuring that a project is accepted and supported.

Related to this point is the inclusion of the people who will be directly impacted by a project in the development of the solution. It is always easier for someone to accept a decision when they had real input into it. A project that is perceived as being conceived by others and is being foisted upon those uninvolved with its making is automatically at a disadvantage and is less likely to achieve success. A project team composition that does not include members of the group that the project is designed to assist is a project team that will be confronted and challenged over and over again.

Project Life Cycles

As a client, it is important for you to appreciate that the project will have a life of its own with arcs of busy engagement and valleys of seemingly little or slow movement. The mistake some clients make is to assume that just because there is not a flurry of activity, that there is not progress being made on the project. Not all project-related activity is necessarily visible to you as the client, especially if the consultant is conducting the work off-site at their own offices.

For any projects other than the most simple, there is likely to be a learning curve where the consultant and the project team sift through and sort out information that is relevant to the project immediately or might have application at some later stage of the project. Especially when the consultant is not very familiar with the personnel within the client organization, there is often a need to acquaint oneself with the various "boxes on the organization chart" and learn the formal job responsibilities these people have, reporting relationships, backgrounds, etc., in addition to the informal relationships these people have with one another (e.g., which executives speak frequently, which executives are likely to disagree, which executives are competing for the same promotion, etc.).

Depending on the complexity of the project and the experience of the consultant, there might be a need to make certain allowances to bring the consultant up to a higher level of proficiency in industry terminology, business processes, equipment or software usage, etc. These decisions around patience or tolerance for longer project times to accommodate a learning curve are typically included in the determination of which consultant to select, and were ideally identified when choosing to go with one consultant over another. Candidly, available budget and costs often determine whether a client can demand excellence immediately or must adjust for the consultant's need to become more expert than he or she already is in the project's requirements.

Given the difficulty of aligning schedules, phases in the project plan that require working with other people within the company or meeting with them for interviews, surveys, or observations often cannot occur as efficiently as would be ideal. This can put pressure on the consultant's ability to conduct all interviews within a certain time frame or might lead to downtime between surveys, observations, etc., as the consultant waits for the next available person to have time to devote to the project.

In other instances, the consultant will have to be very busy juggling multiple phases of the project simultaneously. One recent project of mine had the following people contact me within a 15-minute window:

- Software developers needed assistance in how to "storyboard" links from one section of the software to another
- Users of the software had questions on how the pilot version of the software would change and when they would get to use it
- Course developers wanted to know when they would get copies of the software so that they could create training
- Subject-matter experts wanted to be sure that they were going to be able to approve all changes made to the software
- Client contact asked if we were still on schedule to meet our deadline

And of course, in between all of these were the usual logistical questions of who has yet to be interviewed for their input, when the surveys would be tabulated, who was out sick that day and had to reschedule, etc.

Projects can rarely be completed in an orderly and equally paced way throughout the life of the project. It has been my experience that there will be occasional late nights, weekends, and long days. On the other hand, there are also days where there might be little actual activity, but these brief activities are core to the furtherance of the project. A 15-minute discussion with one particular subject-matter expert might not take all that long to complete, but the implications of that discussion can change the direction and feasibility of a proposed solution and put the project team on a path that will be far superior than what they would have accomplished without the discussion.

It is natural for the project to have peaks and valleys of visible and observable work, but often the work that is being done behind the scenes (research, clarification, flowcharting, etc.) leads to much better solutions and is very necessary to ensure optimal project outcomes. Sometimes this can be confusing for a client that has agreed to a fee or payment schedule that does not quite align with the pacing of the workload on a project. It is not unusual for a project to have three equal payments (beginning, mid-point, end of project), but the client does not see much of anything until the final report. It is quite understandable that the client might feel antsy about having paid two-thirds of the fee without having seen any concrete evidence of performance. The last days/weeks of a project are often filled with activity, and the client wonders why the work could not have been spread out over the duration of the contract or the client thinks that the consultant is unable to manage the project well because there appears to be all this last-minute frenzy of activity. While that might be true, it has been my experience that projects tend to have so-called crunch periods when much needs to be done in a short period of time, and other periods of time where the work is much more evenly handled and there is less urgency.

In my own business, I often view my role as something similar to a chemical catalyst. A chemical catalyst is something that is introduced into an environment and, through its interactions with other chemicals, causes a change to the environment. But unlike other chemicals that are introduced, the catalyst does not become part of the environment itself. It has a direct impact on that environment, but it can be removed wholly from the environment without changing itself. I view consulting to be a similar experience in that it is my intention to create a change to the client's business, but not to become part of that business myself. I need to retain my objectivity and not be blinded by matters that are outside the responsibility or influence of the project. At the end of the project, if I have done the project work correctly and managed the relationship aspects of the assignment appropriately, I can then leave that company having assisted in creating a new environment, but that environment is not dependent on my continuing on in the capacity of consultant for that client. The client is now able to sustain the new environment on its own.

Concrete Versus Abstract Concepts

In working with consultants, the definition and expectation of what will be provided must be clearly understood by all who are integral to the project's success. In some consulting assignments, the consultant will provide direction, guidance, considerations, caveats, or other advice that are meant to then be implemented by the client without further involvement of the consultant. Very often, this kind of consulting is done by so-called "thought leaders" in the industry. The consultant gives you a visionary perspective, shares a series of insights, or provides a new viewpoint, but is not asked to necessarily do anything that is specific to the company or involves anything more than pointing out areas to be addressed within the company. If the client does ask for further assistance in this matter, it is considered a separate project.

The consultant might work with some executives, interview some customers, survey some suppliers, and weave those anecdotes into a presentation, but essentially, the consultant is selling an abstract concept that is now incumbent upon the client to implement. The thinking involved in providing this form of consulting is often revolutionary and shifts paradigms amongst industry captains, but it is often more difficult to measure these forms of consulting. There is an intuitive understanding of what is being provided, but it is harder to truly evaluate and quantify the benefit of this consulting, which does not for a moment mean it is therefore not worthwhile. Quite the contrary, it is often exactly what is needed, but in working with the consultant, it is essential that you, as the client, understand what is being provided and how best to assess its worth.

Other consulting assignments are very tactical and concrete. These projects have a tangible output associated with them. Examples include a training program that will ensure that all attendees can perform with less than 2 errors per 100 transactions, a software application that can accomplish "x," or a succession plan that recognizes the need for diversity in management. At the conclusion of these projects, it is very clear if the objectives were met. Evaluation can occur and measurements can be taken. Either attendees can perform within the tolerance of errors, or they cannot. Either the software performs as expected, or it does not. Either the succession plan provides for diversity in management, or it fails to provide it. In these instances, it is apparent if the project did or did not accomplish the goal.

Execution and Implementation Steps

The challenges confronted by these two forms of consultative assistance differ greatly from each other. In one, the client is left to determine how best to implement the proposed process. In the other, there is at least a road map of how to do it, and often the consultant agrees as part of the assignment to assist in the implementation if it is a training program or some other project that would make sense for the consultant to continue working alongside the client to ensure successful integration into the organization. But although they differ in implementation, they both require attention to be paid to just how the project will be introduced, reinforced, evaluated, and measured by the client organization.

Leaving the implementation to chance is tantamount to accepting that nothing will change. There needs to be a very clearly defined process for how the organization will be expected to integrate the recommendations of the consulting project and begin to perform according to the standards established by the project. Whether this is done jointly with the consultant, alone, or even through the efforts of another consulting resource that is expert at implementation or integration, the client must give careful consideration to just how to ensure that the project is properly executed and implemented.

Checklist for Working with Consultants

1. Have you determined how frequently you will mandate communication related to the project with the consultant? Do you have a plan in place for communicating with and providing feedback to those employees contributing to the project?
2. Do you have a clear conception of what is "in-bounds" to discuss with the consultant (and what is not)?
3. Have you established a method for handling conflict between the consultant and you? Between the consultant and team members? Within team members?
4. Is there a plan in place to sustain interest for the project through wall banners, newsletters, or other means?
5. Have you given thought to the rhythm of the project life cycle and when there is likely to be a flurry of activity and when the project might be seemingly less active (though work is continuing)?

Evaluating a Consultant's Work

Key Learning Points:

- The importance of evaluation
- Ascertaining what to measure
- Determining how to evaluate or assess success
- Importance of post project review or "post mortems"
- Establishment of corporate self-reliance on the consultant's departure or project conclusion
- How to terminate a consulting assignment

One should be careful to get out of an experience only the wisdom that is in it—and stop there; lest we be like the cat that sat down on the hot stove lid! She will never sit down on a hot stove lid again—and that's well; but she also will never sit down on a cold one any more.

— Mark Twain

The last chapter ended with two discussions. The first discussion pointed out the differences between conceptual or abstract consulting services and the more tangible, concrete, and tactical consulting services. This has tremendous implications for how the worth of a consultant and the consultant's efforts is evaluated. The second discussion stressed the importance of leveraging the ideas generated as part of the consulting effort and ensuring that there is some positive action taken within the company to harness the positive potential of those ideas. Without some specific action plan to translate the project's findings or recommendations into definable and specific steps for employees to take, the likelihood of success happening through osmosis is slim. Without the action step being completed to implement or integrate a solution of one kind or another, the ultimate evaluation of the project's success (and therefore, the consultant's efforts) is likely to suffer.

This chapter will examine the components of the evaluative effort and make recommendations on how to best employ an evaluation of the consultant's efforts that are both fair and meaningful to the organization.

Scorecard

My business partner, Jeff Clow, often uses the analogy of a golf scorecard during our training workshops to elucidate the parallels in sports with the business world. He will ask participants if any of them are golfers (typically the participants will give nervous sideways glances to determine if it is "safe" to respond affirmatively or if it will be perceived as an indicator that they are not truly doing their jobs on company time). Once one brave soul admits to spending time or having had experience with golfing, Jeff will ask them what information is contained on the scorecard.

With some occasional prompting, he will draw out that the scorecard used for golf contains:

- A drawing of the layout of the course and specific holes (including measurements or distances to the hole and any obstacles—water hazards, trees, etc.)

- The "par" for the course, or the expected number of strokes required to complete the hole to be considered at a comparable level with a referent group or against a benchmark
- Room to write one's own score on the individual holes
- A place to note the score partway through the course
- A place to tally the scores of the individual holes and determine a cumulative score

Once established and agreed upon by the original brave participant admitting to having golfed before (and all the other duffers in attendance who suddenly remember that they too have spent time on the links), Jeff then engages the class in a dialogue of how similar it is in the business world when evaluating the efforts of a salesperson or service provider:

- Determine through an assessment what the "lay of the land" is or the significance of the issue being confronted. Include obstacles or impediments to success in the assessment, and as appropriate, strategies for overcoming them.
- Establish the objectives for the intervention: Identify what is to be expected as a result of the project.
- Incorporate a device to quantify progress (yields, accuracy, timing, etc.).
- Keep track of or measure performance and progress throughout the project to allow for monitoring, management, and corrective actions as quickly as possible.
- Conclude the project by a critical analysis of performance against the stated or desired outcome. Was the result of the project consistent with what had been expected?

Legitimate Scorecards

In evaluating the performance of the consultant, there are certain approaches or criteria that are more worthwhile than others. Fundamental to good project or consultant evaluation is the understanding that evaluation is not reserved for an "after the fact" review of what transpired over the course of the project or the relationship with the consultant. Evaluation should be embedded into the management of the process on an ongoing basis with frequent confirmations and opportunities for feedback. In a previous section of this book devoted to contracting with the consultant, the recommendation was made to include milestone events periodically throughout the life of the relationship to provide both client and consultant with an opportunity to mutually determine if the project was still a "go" and merited completion, or if the project had lost some of the original intent and should be considered a "no go" or the project is not viable and, therefore, should not be completed.

The lack of surprises between consultant and client in the course of the project is the foundation on which solid relationships can be formed. There should be no reason that a client is unaware of what the status of a project is until the very end. This mid-project scorecard review allows for better monitoring and management of the process and the project, not unlike the score on the golf scorecard tallied at the conclusion of the 9th hole to give the golfer a sense for how well the performance has been to that point against the standard of "par" or according to some "handicap" allowance based on expected outcome.

Any of the following bulleted items should be evaluated through the course of the project:

- Did the consultant correctly assess the project and the difficulties likely to be encountered? Was the consultant permitted to assess the situation, or was the project structured such that the consultant was asked to perform or deliver a result without having had the benefit of "walking the course" one time through to see what the layout of the course included.
- Were the objectives established clearly? Were the objectives consistent throughout the project, or did they change mid-project?
- How are the objectives to be measured? Are the objectives directly tied back to a business issue, or are the objectives of the consultation inconsistent with the goals of the organization?
- Determine the criteria and method for measurement. Quantifiable criteria are easiest to use for comparisons and assessment against expectations, but at times, subjecting a conceptual goal into discrete and measurable units renders an output that is not indicative of the success of the project. For example, if I were to have

as a goal to increase customer satisfaction, it would be tempting to measure the number of customer complaint calls received by the customer service teams. This measurement, though, might not actually be a measurement that accurately reflects customer satisfaction, as a reduction in calls might also mean a reduction in customers and, therefore, fewer people buying the product and fewer complaints—but not at all a positive for the viability of the business long term.

• Include a "debrief" meeting with the consultant. Include what worked and what did not, what about the process used throughout the project facilitated the project and what hindered the project, etc. Give the consultant fair warning that this is your intention and be sure to ask the consultant for input as well (and not just rely on insights derived from internal employees).

Irresponsible Scorecards

Upon occasion in my consulting practice, I will meet with other consultants at industry functions or association meetings. At these meetings, consultants will occasionally share amongst themselves how they have been evaluated by clients on a basis that seemed not only wrong-headed, but irresponsible (that combination laughter and moaning that you hear at the hotel lounge might be another group of consultants comparing notes). While I stubbornly cling to the belief that the clients were not making the evaluative decisions with the intent of being irresponsible, the end result was a client organization that suffered the consternation of a project gone bad, an unhappy client contact, and the loss of future business for the consultant with that client.

Some of the approaches that consultants have shared with me on misaligned scorecards or evaluative criteria are:

• **"Smile sheets."** Those quick and dirty evaluations that are passed out as the consultant completes a presentation or speech often contain the following rigorous and meaningful criteria: Was the room temperature comfortable? Did the catering meet your needs? Did the consultant introduce herself to you satisfactorily?

A presentation attendee running for the next meeting or trying to leave a training session to catch an earlier flight home is not typically in the right mindset to provide quality evaluative feedback. So instead, why not have the attendee *and* the manager of the attendee where appropriate assess the change in skills or approach or behavior (*action* orientation) as a result of the training or presentation? As a consultant, I am less concerned with being "liked" for how I introduce myself to a meeting attendee than I am about whether the meeting attendee leaves my session with a better or more comprehensive skill set.

I wonder if the influences of MTV, Sesame Street, and other media offerings have blinded both clients and consultants to the real "meat" of the project—results. Rather than focusing on the results, we are holding each other accountable for "entertainment" value of the project (Was it comfortably conducted? Did you enjoy it? Would you do it again? etc.). All too often, the evaluation focuses on the peripheral issues of client comfort (not to discount them entirely, but they are not the purpose of the project).

- **"Are we there yet?"** In the urgency to achieve and accomplish objectives, it is sometimes the case that due to quarterly pressures or other demands for results, clients will expect to see the impact of results in the very short term. When the project is something that can be accomplished sooner rather than later, it might be beneficial to apply pressure to get things done immediately. It can serve to galvanize activity and provide focus to efforts.

  However, as often as I have seen the above scenario lead to positive outcomes, the rush to accomplish the task has relegated the project to little more than a "check off" on the to-do list of some executive. The project's intent is lost in the desire to get it completed. The attention to detail, desire to "do it right," and intent to transfer the meaningfulness of the effort to others within the organization are sacrificed at the expense of being able to "put the project to bed." Sadly, the efforts expended on the project will be for naught, and the project's original intent will still be unsatisfied, only now it will have to overcome a hurdle of having been previously addressed and not resulting in an improved situation. Therefore, it might be harder to get time and attention paid to it to address the original issue since it runs the risk of being accepted as a "cost of doing business around here."

- **"Do-it-for-me-itis."** One of the surest ways to trip up a consulting project's likelihood for success is for the consultant to assume sole responsibility for (or for the client to hold the consultant accountable for) the project's success. Similar to the craze found in dieting and fitness, too many clients want a "quick fix" that is painless and does not require effort on their part. The analogy of a magic elixir, surgery, or some other panacea is preferred by the executive to the hard work of having to actually perform in a newly disciplined way to change results. Unfortunately, some consultants will step into this breech and overcommit and overpromise that they can change results *for* the client (not assist, guide, or direct, but rather complete the changes on behalf of the client). Any project that has as its performance outcome or expectation that the consultant will perform some feat of magic without the client having to be fully engaged in the work of achieving that outcome is a project doomed to fail.

  For a client to see the results and output of a consulting project, the better model to use is to view the consultant as a personal trainer. Like a personal trainer, the consultant might direct the efforts of the client team, monitor, encourage, correct, or a whole host of other activities to bring the client to a desired state—but at no time does the personal trainer lift the weights, run the miles, or complete the exercise *for* the person seeking a higher level of fitness.

- **Misaligned objectives.** A project that purports to be about one objective, but is truly being measured on the merits of another objective, is a project that will likely fail to achieve either objective. A company that I am familiar with hired a consultant with much internal fanfare to streamline their processes and increase efficiencies between and among different departments, functions, and even across country borders to reduce waste, redundancies of parallel information systems, and other inefficiencies. To make the project seem rather important and give it an aura of mystery, they even gave it a special name (down the path of "Project Gamma Ray"). This company then had the consultant interview, observe, analyze, and assess employees. Much of the process of the project seemed to be focused on trimming head count and not at all on really changing processes. Obviously, it should come as no surprise that the employees quickly came to distrust the process, the consultant, and management, and in short order, the rumor mill further created even greater tales of management's true intent and the impending apocalypse for employees.

While management scratched their heads at the surge of employee resignations to accept other jobs, the outcome was that the project's lone "benefit" as listed in their annual report was a reduction in workforce and the associated savings that generated. But the implications of the assignment were much deeper—the "best and brightest" were the ones who left, and the remaining employees were mostly those who were unable to find or seek other jobs (either through life circumstances or lack of desirability on the open market). At last report, the company was in such dire straits that it was seeking to be acquired by a deep-pocketed "white knight" to infuse enough capital to right the wrongs of the prior administration.

In measuring or evaluating the success or lack of success of a consultant's efforts, be sure to be clear on:

- What the outcome should look like or how you will recognize success
- What the timing will be for achieving success
- What the responsibility of the consultant will be, and what the responsibility of the company/client will be
- What has been/is being communicated about the project (formal and informal), what that communication consists of, and if that is consistent with what the project is truly designed to accomplish (employees, stockholders, and other interested parties can be fooled only for so long before they can begin to sniff out if something is rotten)

Quantitative Evaluation

The most direct way to evaluate a consultant's work is to take a very specific measurement pre-intervention, and then take one post-intervention, the assumption being that the only thing that changed between those two measurements is the work of the consultant and the resultant effect of the project. Of course, that is never exactly true in the orthodoxy of scientific and statistical analysis. Consultants and clients rarely have the benefit of being able to conduct their work in settings resembling laboratories where other variables can be controlled and prevented from impacting results; regardless of the project, competitors will continue to affect market conditions, employees will come and go, economic conditions will change, and consumers will evolve and change their behaviors. Nevertheless, the closest many consultants and clients can come to measuring the impact of a project and the efforts of the consultant still resides with a quantitative measurement taken before the project commences and sometime after it has been completed.

There are certain evaluative criteria that lend themselves nicely to a quantitative measurement:

- Number of processing errors within a time period
- Speed to market with a new item
- Duration of new hires remaining with the company
- Accuracy of key punch operators
- Number of calls handled

As mentioned in the previous section, any and all of these can lead to decisions being made that might actually be counter-productive to the welfare and benefit of the organization. For example, if number of calls handled is the metric used to determine success of a project, it is not hard to project that the motivation to handle multiple calls in a short period of time might lead to less-effective assistance being offered on any one call. Since the measurement of calls handled does not capture accuracy or thoroughness of assistance offered, the call handlers will provide higher "throughput" of calls being handled, but at a potential decrease in the quality of any individual call.

Qualitative

The other side of the evaluation coin is the qualitative assessment, which is less easily and objectively measured by a clock, ruler, or other accepted metric. In my experience as a consultant, the qualitative is perhaps even more important than the quantitative in developing a long-term consulting relationship between client and consultant. Ironic as it might seem, clients and consultants will "explain away" the quantitative to suit their purposes ("Poor results were not a result of poor project design by the consultant, but poor execution by the field," or "Lack of increase in sales volume was directly linked to declining market share of product due to customer consolidation," etc.). However, even if a project did deliver successful quantitative measures, if the consultant was difficult to work with, did not communicate well with client contacts, or lacked a host of other "softer skills" that interfered with the project's qualitative aspects, it is a safe bet that the consultant and client will no longer work together from that point forward.

Earlier, I scoffed at the importance of "introducing myself appropriately" to meeting attendees. It might seem now that I am contradicting myself by highlighting the importance of the qualitative aspects. The difference is between what "should be" important and what "is" important. The true value of the consultant's efforts *should* be in things other than what could pejoratively be called "buying a friend" (smiling, polite conversation, enjoyable personality, etc.). Most of us, if confronted with choosing a surgeon who was bereft of social skills, but an excellent practitioner, would choose that person over someone who was kind and friendly, but less skilled. If the choices include someone who possesses *both* social skills and professional competence, then clearly it is that person who should be selected. Yet, all too often, clients will choose based on, and consultants will focus on, the skills of being amiable, affable, and easy to get along with. Unfortunately, this leads to a mediocrity of effort as the consultant is fearful of pushing the envelope past what the client is prepared to accept in the way of suggestions, and the client rebuffs attempts to do anything beyond the most conventional and conservative approaches to projects (even at the expense of ensuring the project is destined to fail).

While I cannot change the direction of the industry and the relationships between consultants and clients, you, the reader/client, can. While you might not apply as high a "weight" to qualitative factors as the quantitative, just by virtue of measuring them, holding the consultant accountable for them, and ensuring that you evaluate the consultant on the following evaluative criteria, you will have done your part to improve the evaluation of consulting services, and the benefit of what you receive from that consultant:

- Did the consultant communicate clearly with you? With all members of the project team?
- Did the consultant communicate in a timely fashion (no surprises at the last minute)?
- Did the consultant challenge accepted ideas or practices and offer potential alternatives?
- Did the consultant work to understand your organization, or provide just a generic solution that could easily fit any organization?
- Did the consultant suggest other/better ways of determining impact/benefit of project outcome?
- Was the consultant attentive to your requests or unique needs throughout the project?
- Were all consultants assigned to the project properly briefed and qualified to work on the project (or were there consultants who seemed to slow down the progress of the project due to their own limitations)?
- Was the consultant who "sold" the project involved in the project work, or was he/she only a "figure head" who was more focused on selling the project's follow-up once the original project was signed?
- Did the consultant meet all deadlines?
- Did the consultant maintain confidences and not divulge secrets?
- Was the consultant willing to take direction and accept decisions made by the project team/key client contacts?
- Was the consultant capable/willing to work as part of a team, or was the consultant pursuing an individual agenda?
- Was the consultant more concerned with generating leads, securing the next project, or working on the existing project?

As you can see from the above list (which is by no means exhaustive), the elements of the consulting relationship that are separate and distinct from the consultant's competence in the area of subject-matter expertise can overwhelm and overshadow that ability in the eyes of a client. Failure to connect with a client on the "soft skills" side of consulting is a ticket to immediate expulsion and an invitation to not return to that client again.

Your Role

While the expectations of the consultant should be discussed beforehand, it is often appropriate and necessary to consider having intermediate meetings or conversations to discuss how closely aligned the client's expectations and the consultant's behavior are through the course of the project or assignment. In my experience, at the end of an engagement, both client and consultant are moving forward onto other assignments, and rarely take the time to assess the project and determine what worked well and what did not.

But the benefit to you, the client, of making the time to conduct these "post mortems" is that you gain greater insight into what your strengths are from a project management perspective. The advantage you derive from analyzing how the project's success was fostered or hampered by your actions (or the unanticipated actions of others) is of paramount importance to your own career success. Ask yourself, "How well did I:

- Explain the goals and objectives of the project to the consultant?"
- Critically assess the consultant's skills and experience/background through the proposal process?"
- Communicate and provide feedback (positive or negative) to the consultant?"
- Communicate within my own organization to explain the purpose of the consultant's efforts?"
- Provide the consultant with appropriate access to subject-matter experts within my company that could aid in the project's accuracy/efficiency/effectiveness?"

- Maintain deadlines for reviews of materials submitted by the consultant and keep to schedules originally agreed upon?"
- Keep appropriate controls on costs, spending, or other project-related financial matters?"

One of the dilemmas in working with consultants and evaluating their contribution to a project is that it is often hard to separate the person from the work product. Evaluating the person's output as distinct from the personality or approach used by the person is recommended. Clearly, both are important and either can torpedo a project. However, though competence or expertise can overcome a poor match of personalities, affability cannot triumph over incompetence. If given the choice to work with a surly accountant who has proven her worth to you in savings of thousands of dollars over the course of a year versus working with someone you look forward to speaking to and laughing with, but has yet to contribute to your bottomline, most of us would opt for the less-personable accountant.

Therefore, it is recommended that when you assess the project and the consultant, you divide the evaluation into those variables that are person-related and those that are skill-related. After doing that, you can then decide just how much credence or value to place on each of those factors in making your decisions for future business with consultants.

Above all, keep a firm grasp on how well the project and consultant delivered the intended outcomes or objectives. While the process might not have been pleasant at all times, neither is surgery. Yet, most of us would agree that the successful result of having a surgical procedure far outweighs the pain or stress of rehabilitation. The more aligned the evaluation is with the original or intended objectives, the better the assessment of the project and the consultant.

One Last Word on Relationships

While a consultant is a "gun for hire" or an expert called upon to assist you based on their expertise, and the hope is that the person is someone of high moral fiber and virtue, there is a dark side to the process that must be addressed so that you are forewarned and can be on the lookout for it.

Most consultants are objective people who genuinely want what is best for the client company and endeavor to contribute their efforts toward the client's betterment. Given the choice between purposely leading the client astray and assisting the client to achieve an appropriate objective, it is clear that the consultant will seek to deliver the positive outcome. Where this scenario sometimes becomes muddy is when two variables are introduced to the situation:

1. Consultant as businessperson
2. Ambiguity

The consultant is employed (either by a firm or self-employed) to provide services to clients, but is also a businessperson him- or herself. Few consultants can afford to provide their services without some remuneration in exchange, nor do they have any interest in doing so. When a consultant has to choose between providing what is asked for by a client and providing what is "right" for the client (in the opinion of that consultant), it can often come down to a decision that factors in the amount of the fee for each option. It takes someone with a strong conviction about being objective and putting the client's needs ahead of one's own to stare down the barrel of that gun and suggest that the client not pay the consultant for services that are being requested, but not needed.

Many consultants feel they are beholden to a standard that exceeds a mere Profit and Loss Statement (P&L) (which is easier said than done when the P&L is not positive!), and thankfully, the instances of consultants intentionally deluding clients into spending money unnecessarily is not as common as one would fear (or the trust given to consultants would suffer dramatically). However, let's not lose sight of the fact that the consultant is running a business, and that business is dependent on the same factors as any other business: revenue, cash flow, operational efficiencies, labor utilization, etc.

A consultant might even rationalize their choice to sell unnecessary additional projects or projects that are not necessarily needed by claiming, "The client wanted it," or "While it might not have helped, it did not hurt anything, so why not do it?"

Consultants are salespeople; they happen to sell a service or a so-called "intangible" as opposed to a product, but they still sell. Many sales training efforts include some variation of the following suggestion:

"Make friends with your buyer."

The thinking goes that if the client is someone who views you as a "friend," then it is that much easier to sell future projects, and it is that much harder to disengage from one another. After all, who wants to fire a friend, and don't most of us prefer to work with someone we view as a friend? With that in mind, the consultant will often try to improve the relationship status they have with you (through gifts, interest in your hobbies or pursuits away from the office, or offers to meet out of the office over meals or at a show or a ball game). While the consultant might be ethical and there might not be an attempt on their part to do anything beyond sharing a meal or an event, others might view this more cynically. Pay attention to your "antenna" on this one. If it seems too elaborate or not in keeping with the parameters of the relationship, it might be an attempt by the consultant to "win" future business from you on the strength of a friendship or the hope that you will feel as if you "owe" that consultant due to their having entertained you.

Harsh Realities

The opposite end of the spectrum is the consultant's charge to occasionally deliver what my business partner, Jeff Clow, refers to as "the unpleasant truths and harsh realities." While all of us much prefer to hear that we are doing a wonderful job and that our efforts are positive, the consultant might be put in a position of having to share with a client contact that their efforts are negatively impacting the business' performance.

A consultant confronted with the challenge of sharing information that is distasteful to the receiver will fear retribution and might attempt to "soften" or even ignore it. Not wanting to risk a "shoot the messenger" situation, the consultant might opt to not deliver the message and protect future business. Of course, a consultant who does not provide that input is not doing a service to either the client or their own business in the long term, but those concerns are often neglected or mitigated by immediate business pressures and fears of reprisals.

Prior to starting a career in consulting, I worked as a full-time employee under a man whose approach to conflict management and problem solving was lifted off of Hollywood's version of a drill sergeant.

He would bark at, threaten, and intimidate anyone who dared to question one of his decisions. After numerous run-ins with various subordinates, he stopped receiving the input of his corporate lieutenants. When he erupted yet again about why he was not briefed on something that was occurring, he was told that no one wanted to risk the confrontation that was sure to occur upon his being told of a plan that was not exactly as he wished. When he shouted that he was now even more upset than he would have otherwise been, and asked the brave subordinate whether it was worth his ire now, the subordinate said, "Yes, because while you are upset now, we did not have to deal with your anger the last four times we made a decision without running it by you."

Jeff Clow, prior to co-founding the firm that bears our name, was president of a division for a leading market research firm. He had been asked to attend a meeting with other senior executives of the company to discuss communication styles, perceptions of others and their impact on behavior, and how to maximize the productivity of cross-division efforts. He came back from that session with new-found insights into how powerful feedback can be and how meaningful hearing others' perceptions of him is in shaping his approaches. This is a lesson he has applied within our firm to lead and direct executives who have not had the benefit of hearing the unvarnished truth about themselves and their actions.

As a client, you can only do so much to overcome this (not many clients seek or solicit feedback that is critical of themselves), but being keenly aware of how the consultant approaches difficult conversations or handles potentially controversial assignments can give you some insight into whether the consultant is capable of delivering the "unpleasant truths and harsh realities."

Next Steps

As mentioned previously, the consultant is often intent on securing future contracts with you and will attempt to sell additional projects to you as the existing one is coming to a close. Ideally, the scope of projects should be agreed upon upfront, and any follow-up projects or phased assignments would have been identified initially. You are relying on the consultant as an expert to give you a "landscape view" of the immediate and future needs based on the current position or skills of your company. While it is at times a scary proposition for that consultant to constantly be pushed out of the nest and asked to go fly away or at least to the next assignment, that is not your primary concern as a client (nor should it even be your secondary concern).

From a consultant's perspective, projects that have "scope creep" are to be closely managed to prevent a client from adding additional requests into the original contract without additional fees or cost. On the other side of the coin, clients need to be vigilant that as contracts or projects conclude, they don't fall prey to a consultant's attempt to elongate or extend an engagement through additional project work (clients are especially vulnerable if the consultant is on a retainer basis or there is no clearly defined start and stop to the contract).

Upon occasion, things will be learned during the execution of the project that were unanticipated, or there are outcomes that neither the client nor the consultant could foresee during the initial contracting for the project. In those instances, there might be application for extension of the project and continuance of payments; however, these should be the exception and not the rule for most situations. A consultant who extends the contract on the same or related projects without having given the client some advance notice of the future need to do so is probably acting in his or her own best interests and not those of the client.

As mentioned in the discussion about proposals and contracting, it is perfectly acceptable and recommended that projects include multi-year plans and phased implementations that are scheduled to commence upon completion of the most immediate phase or stage of a project. I am not taking issue with long-term relationships between consultants and clients. What I am alerting you to is the practice among some unscrupulous consultants of trying to build their client's dependence upon them and, in so doing, ensuring that there is a steady stream of income for as long as the ruse survives.

Teach Me to Fish

The best consultants have to do something rather unusual in today's business environment: They have to work themselves out of a job.

With tongue firmly planted in cheek, one perspective is that the best work a consultant can do is to make themselves obsolete and no longer necessary to the client.

A consultant and client should agree on whether there is a desire for the client to "learn how to fish" as opposed to "having the consultant fish for them." On that basis then, a decision can be made as to whether the consultant and the client can work harmoniously together. To use a medical analogy, there are certain steps that a client can take to "self-medicate" or to ensure that they maintain the proper conditions for corporate results (instead of rest and nutrition, the client might substitute career pathing, technology, etc.).

As a client, you have a right to ask your consultant to explain methodologies and processes employed in executing a project. Just as a medical technician or physician shows you an X-ray or radiograph, or provides test results prior to a medical procedure, your consultant should share what diagnostics were employed, why a suggested approach is best, and what one can reasonably expect to occur as a result of the intervention. The other side of the coin is that the consultant fears that sharing much or any of this might result in the client choosing to do it on their own and the consultant losing the client's business for the future. Then again, these fears can be allayed to some extent if the consultant analogizes this situation as a medical one: How many of us are willing to do surgery on ourselves no matter how much we understand or have had the procedure explained to us?

Willing to Use Again

If you have made the decision to use the consultant again or are at least open to having the consultant work with you in the future, then take the time to let the consultant know that and what they need to improve upon to further provide value to you. If you have decided *not* to use the consultant again, it would be a kindness to share that as well and explain why not. While less critical or vital to your business to let the consultant know they are not going to be retained, the lessons learned will be valuable for the consultant and might help shape your future decisions as you are more aware of what you do *not* want. In either case, documenting what worked and what did not will help guide your subsequent projects with consultants and will help formulate the preferences of you and your company (in companies where there is a "preferred vendor list" this is very important information to feed back into the process to ensure that it is maintained and is current with the latest information).

As consulting projects are most often assigned based on recommendations or personal contact and not through advertisements or mass-marketing attempts, the consultant might request a reference from you or might ask you to be available to talk with future prospects or clients of that consulting firm. You are under no obligation to do so, and I have heard of consultants and clients using that as a bartered or negotiated tactic to reduce future fees (it seems morally gray to me to leverage a recommendation or reference from one client without disclosing to the prospect that there is a quid pro quo or benefit being derived for the reference). I choose *not* to trade fees for references and believe that if it were possible, there should be a disclaimer that scrolls across the e-mail or telephone call that announces that the person providing the reference is a "paid spokesperson" for the consulting company.

If you are willing to give a reference and are thrilled with the service or results offered by the consultant, then, by all means, shout it from the rooftops and let everyone know; the consultant will thank you and the prospect will appreciate your insight. If you are dissatisfied and want to use this opportunity to "get back" at the consultant, then I would strongly advise you to reconsider. Let the consultant know you are uncomfortable speaking favorably about the project or the consultant's contribution and why you cannot in good conscience provide a favorable recommendation. The consultant will appreciate that much more than having you rail against the consulting services offered to a prospect, and most prospects would be confused by your negative assessment anyway (Why is this person so negative? What is the motivation for the attack? etc.). While you might be upset by the result of a consulting project, remember that this is how the consultant makes a living, and while I am not at all an apologist for the incompetent consultants among us, I am one who prefers to educate my clients to make a more informed choice and then let the market dictate whether a consultant has what it takes to generate sufficient project work to stay in business.

Firing a Consultant

Even after you have taken all of the steps outlined in this book to ensure you have done everything you could to stave off the termination of a consulting relationship (though, more likely, termination will occur more frequently when steps to this point have been missed or glossed over), it might at times be necessary to end a consulting relationship prior to a project's conclusion.

If you recall from the proposals and contracts discussion, I suggested integrating a series of go/no-go steps into the process. Those steps were designed to provide both sides with an opportunity to assess whether it made sense to continue the project or the business relationship. You might also remember that communication and feedback have been stressed throughout the book to allow for ample opportunity to address any necessary issues that develop and make any mid-course corrections as identified. In the event that a no-go decision is reached, the project and consulting assignment can end as contractually agreed upon. In the event that there has been an issue that has arisen that requires immediate attention, the emphasis on communication throughout the process and on feedback ordinarily provides the two sides with the opportunity to agree on an approach (or to agree that there is not enough common ground, and therefore, it no longer makes sense to continue the relationship).

When "firing" or failing to retain the consultant further, it has been my experience that you will best protect yourself if the following is done (this is not meant to constitute legal or financial advice; seek counsel of trusted advisors and experts before taking these steps):

1. Let the consultant know of the decision (best if done in writing and according to whatever stipulations were agreed upon contractually) and when it will take effect.
2. Collect any information, proprietary programs, software, drawings, diagrams, manuals, etc., that were shared in the course of the project to that point.

3. Ensure that other non-collected materials are destroyed since corporate espionage by competitors or just those who are curious has made just throwing materials in the trash a less secure method of removing trade secrets or strategically important documents from the possession of the consultant.

4. Ensure that any outstanding invoices, expense reports, or other monies owed are transacted and paid in full (should there be disputes about fees or expenses, be sure to document what is not being paid and why).

5. If there is a transition of the project to another consultant, be sure that any original consultant proprietary materials are *not* shared with the second consulting firm (you want to avoid any legal imbroglios or even the hint of one).

6. Explain the decision to those internal employees working on the project to the extent of a "need to know" basis and keep the information shared to facts and not taking gratuitous swipes at the consultant. Share how the project will be continued and what will be expected of the team members.

Checklist for Evaluating the Consulting Relationship

1. Have you chosen appropriate criteria and metrics for evaluating the project's success? Do those chosen criteria and metrics support or compete with the intended outcomes of the project?

2. Have you communicated to the consultant what will be the criteria for evaluating the success of the project and of the consultant's efforts?

3. Do you have a way of distinguishing what is an evaluation of the consultant's performance as differentiated from the consultant's personality or other noncompetency-based criteria that are worthy of inclusion in the evaluation?

4. Do you have a post mortem scheduled to review your evaluation with all relevant participants (consultant, team members, subject-matter experts who contributed to the project, etc.)?

5. Is there a plan in place to assume ongoing control for the project beyond the consultant's departure? Is the organization prepared

to be self-reliant enough at the conclusion of the project to continue deriving the benefits of the consulting project?

6. If necessary, have you correctly handled the termination of the
consultant and ensured that there is a minimization of disruption
to the company, the project, and the ability to achieve the desired
goal through other means?

Exiting the Consulting Relationship

Key Learning Points:

- Ending the consulting relationship positively
- Handling the transition to project management without the consultant's involvement
- Concluding all administrative or contractual obligations
- Determining whether to externally publicize the project and the relationship through advertisements, public relations efforts, or industry conferences

Everybody, soon or late, sits down to a banquet of consequences.
— Robert Louis Stevenson

What should be clear by now is that much of the consultant's effort to this point has been focused on not only securing the initial assignment, but also on developing your dependency as a client on that consultant's services. Wherever and whenever possible, the consultant might look to create a perceived need for his or her services on an ongoing, or at least repetitive, basis. From the consultant's point of view, an existing client is always easier than a prospect to convert into a future client. The existing client has already cleared a number of hurdles:

1. They have a bias toward using outside assistance (as proven by the existing consulting relationship). This is often one of the toughest things for a consultant to overcome: the prospect that refuses to consider hiring an outsider.

2. They have budget for the use of outside resources. It is not sufficient for the prospect to have a desire or an interest to use external resources; they need to be funded or have budget to accommodate the use of consultants. An existing client, by virtue of their having already used a consultant, proves that they do have the ability to fund the use of expert talent for identified needs. Of course, the consultant has to battle the limited funds or "dry well" eventuality. Companies will not have unending ability to fund projects, but from a consultant's point of view, if services were funded previously, there is a better-than-even chance that there will be additional funds available to "tap into" either immediately or sometime in the near future.

3. The consultant has managed to secure the first assignment, and in so doing, has proven that the prospect/client has chosen and might tend to choose again that consultant to perform work on their behalf. The second assignment is often seen as his or hers to lose, since the consultant now has the inside track and can build equity or curry favor with decision makers and budget handlers from the perspective of an "insider." This is a highly leveraged tool for a consultant. The initial investment of time, money, and resources to bring a new consultant up to the same level of understanding as the existing consultant about the project, the unique culture of the company, and any political situations in many instances will sway the prospect to just stick with the existing consultant and roll any subsequent phases of the existing project or any new project assignments to that consultant. When consultants get together to share insights about client relationship building and sales, they will

remind each other that the key to consulting is to sell the third project, not the first. Your consultant is likely looking to remain with you a good long time and will investigate avenues within your company to stay well past the conclusion of that first project.

Conclusion of Working Relationship

In speaking with clients and consultants, they will only half jokingly refer to the end of the assignment as the time when the client has to leave the consultant, and not the other way around. As projects reach their natural conclusion, the client has to that point developed a dependency on that consultant (real or imagined), and often, strong relationships have been forged. The client has a momentary fear that without the consultant's presence, the good work that has been done to that point will not be sustainable. This often leads to extensions and new phases of project roll-outs that are profitable for the consultant, but amount to little more than hand-holding and babysitting. The client is unwilling or unable to assume control of the project and its execution in the absence of the consultant, and so like a new bird that refuses to leave the nest, it relies on the consultant to keep feeding it even after it is perfectly capable of doing so itself.

As a client, you will want to be sure within your own mind as to what you expect of the relationship. Is this a project-based relationship, or are you seeking a longer-term resource? Do you wish to encourage the continuation of the consultant's services past the project? How willing are you to control the access the consultant has to others within your company to ensure that you remain "in control" of that consultant's exposure to the company?

If you are prepared to end the relationship with the consultant due to the conclusion of the project and seeing no further use of the consultant's services (at least in the immediate foreseeable future), then you want to ensure that the following occur:

- Final "deliverable" is completed
- Return of all materials
- Destruction of files and materials as required
- Suggested "next steps"

Final Deliverable

The final "deliverable" or the step recognized as the conclusion of the project, a presentation of findings, an execution of a workshop, a report on recommendations, or an analysis, etc., must be delivered (hence, the name "deliverable") or completed by the consultant. The parameters of that last step must be clearly spelled out. Specifics to be identified are:

1. What is the step that denotes the conclusion of the consulting project? Failure to identify when the project will be completed is likely to result in disagreements, extended projects (and possibly fees), and a sense of lack of closure.
2. What is the acceptable level of performance for that concluding step? Is it a report, a presentation, a product?
3. What is the standard that final step (and the project in total) must meet? Is it a comparison between competitors, is it a process that shaves two days off of account receivable posting, or is it recommendations for future strategy or a vision statement?
4. What is the timing of the final step or "deliverable"? Is there a specific date that the project will be concluded by, or is it contingent upon other steps that are non-date dependent being completed first before the final step can be executed?

Return of All Materials

Another important consideration when concluding a project is the return of all materials related to the project that the client company might have provided to the consultant over the course of the project. It is not uncommon to have a project that is better facilitated or accomplished by sharing proprietary information with the consultant. Understanding that most ethical consultants would abide by their agreements not to use that access or information with a direct competitor to the client company, it is still incumbent upon the client to retrieve those materials at project conclusion. It is infinitely better not to leave that to chance or risk misunderstandings at what is in "public domain" and, therefore, usable by the consultant on another project, and what is confidential and proprietary.

Destruction of Files and Materials

Most consulting contracts include a clause limiting the consultant from working with competing clients for a period of time, and prohibiting the use of any company-specific information not currently readily available from other public sources with other clients or on other projects outside the client company. To minimize the exposure or risk that a client has of having their strategic information shared with those that they themselves have not authorized to have access to, it is best to reclaim all materials that have been shared with the consultant.

In some instances, the information might have been shared electronically via e-mail, or through Internet connections. It is not practical to ask for the return of a copy of information that could easily be copied and stored for future use. In those instances (and frankly, the same goes for easily copied paper documents), it is standard practice to insist that the consultant sign a document agreeing that all files and electronic information that had been shared in the course of the consulting project have been deleted, destroyed, or returned. While this is no fail-safe to ensure that an employee of the consulting firm has not kept a copy of confidential materials, it does reinforce your seriousness about maintaining controls over your own materials. The threat of legal action against a consulting firm for violation of that agreement is frightening enough for most consulting firms to prevent too many abuses from occurring. No consultant wants to gamble their future employment with other clients by having their name sullied by accusations of unethical behavior or risk being perceived as untrustworthy. The trust and faith that clients and prospects put in their consultants is too strong to have most consultants willingly jeopardize it.

Suggested Next Steps

In speaking with clients and consultants, one of the steps that cause each the most consternation is the lack of suggested "next steps." As the project reaches its natural conclusion, and the final deliverable for the project is completed, there should be a recommendation of what to do next by the client (or by the consultant). Rather than assuming that the client knows what to do, the consultant needs to provide a map or a plan to accomplish the goal of the project. Clearly, this is going to vary by the project and how the client and consultant envisioned the original scope. Even given those wide differences, however, there are still occasions where the client sees the outcome clearly (based on the consultant's work, or their own ability to recognize what "should be" versus "what is"), but is less sure of how to get from their current situation to that goal on the horizon.

A smart client will have recognized what steps are worth taking in-house and doing with internal resources, and what steps require the assistance of the consultant to accomplish the goal. It is only then that the client can remain truly in control of the process. Allowing a consultant to dictate the next steps for a client is tantamount to handing over the keys to the kingdom and hoping for the best. At all times, you as the client must be sure that you are clear on what the overarching goals of the project are, and how to best use your resources to achieve that (using either internal or external resources).

Many consultants will want to extend their relationship with you for as long as they can. They will seek other projects and add steps to the existing one in an effort to continue the relationship. While occasionally these might be appropriate and consist of good counsel, be very diligent in assessing the merit of any of these suggestions. The consultant might be in a position to advise you based on the experience and exposure with your company to take additional steps to ensure success of the project, or to leverage a situation or opportunity that presented itself during the current phase of the project. However, be wary of project add-ons that appear to be of little value, and conclude the existing project as planned where and when it appears that the value contracted for has been received.

Administrative Responsibilities

Many clients have shared with me that their least favorite aspect of the relationship with consultants is the administrative responsibility. Consultants, by virtue of their not being internal employees, introduce a level of complexity for some corporate managers that they otherwise would not have to confront. Working with a consultant typically requires some steps of administration and tracking/follow-through that would not be needed with an employee:

- Initial payments/setting up vendor/tax forms
- Hours tracking
- Expense payments
- Mid-project status reports
- Scheduling meetings
- Final payment

Payments

Many consultants will require an initial payment prior to or close to the commencement of project work. In order to accommodate that demand, client contacts will often have to complete various internal processes designed to establish that vendor in the client's accounts payable roster of accepted and approved vendors. Among the steps required for that vendor might be:

- Providing the vendor's federal tax identification number. This is especially important if the vendor is working under the W-9 tax form requirements. For additional information on this distinction, seek counsel from an accountant or attorney well versed in business law and contracting with independent vendors.
- Offering any minority or disabled status the vendor might have (some clients want to demonstrate that they are non-discriminatory in their hiring practices, and others receive benefits for using disadvantaged firms as suppliers or vendors).
- Submitting the signed contract and any legal approvals required by the client company.

This up-front work can often delay or stall the beginning of projects, therefore, a consultant will often agree to start a project under the agreement with their client contact that it will all be taken care of prior to the conclusion of the project. In the natural course of events, the project might actually begin "under the radar screen" of the corporate management, and the client contact might forget or is slow to get the right paperwork processed. As long as the consultant is agreeable and perceives there is a better-than-even chance that there will be future business with you as the client, there will not be much to complain about (especially if the payments are being received and the other paperwork is seen as "nice to have" but not essential by the client contact or the consultant.). However, all that will change as soon as the project is slated to conclude and there are still outstanding issues to be addressed by either the client or the consultant. Suddenly, what seemed less important becomes critical. Therefore, it is in everyone's best interests that paperwork and administrative requirements be completed to the satisfaction of each party in as timely fashion as possible to prevent the end-of-project rush to get those things accomplished.

Hours Tracking

Consulting projects come in many varieties. Some clients much prefer the pay-by-the-hour approach where only the consultant hours applied to the project are billed, and an accounting of who did the work and how much work in hours was done is provided to the client contact. While this allows for close monitoring and supervision of the budget and of the work provided, it also creates the need to complete forms that track the project hours and work completed on the consultant's side, and the necessity to review it on the client side.

If the project is to be billed by the "consultant hour" or by the "day," then the accurate tracking of all project-related work should be done prior to final payments being provided to the consultant. Having a schedule of when those work logs of time devoted to the project are to be provided to the client contact can help facilitate the smooth conclusion of the project. Waiting for the last minute to ask for this information, or from the consultant's perspective, waiting for the last minute to provide it, opens up the possibilities of forgetting the time devoted to key components of the project; arguments about who did what, when, and for how long; and discord when it could have easily been avoided had there been a more regular schedule established.

Expenses

During the course of the project, it is not at all uncommon for the consultant to incur expenses that will need to be reimbursed. Certain contracts call for a flat fee reimbursement (a percentage of the contract), and others are on an "as incurred" basis. For the expenses that are to be reimbursed as they are incurred, it is often required that specific forms detailing the expenses be submitted with original receipts attached or any other back-up necessary to validate the expense. In either case, it behooves both the consultant and the client to complete all the necessary reimbursements and collection of expenses prior to the official completion of the project, or as near to it as possible.

Status Reports

Given that many projects comprise multiple phases and there might be a series of go/no-go steps included when the consultant and the client discuss the project's progress and make decisions on whether it is still appropriate to proceed with the original agreement of the project, the need for status reports or updates is essential. These reports can be as formal or as informal as required to ensure that there are no surprises between client and consultant, but at the same time, need to communicate the necessary information required to make an informed decision about the progress of the project. At minimum, these reports typically include the following information:

- Work completed
- Consultants involved in work
- Result of work completed
- Phase of the project
- Objectives of the phase/expected outcome or results
- Any variance of actual result from expectation
- Obstacles or hurdles encountered that were unexpected/explanation of why variance occurred
- Suggested next steps
- Impact on the project (timing, budget, or other aspects)

There is no specific format for status reports—they can even be handwritten—but there must be effective communication between consultant and client to ensure that the project progress is monitored throughout. This becomes essential upon the conclusion of the project to prevent any last minute surprises from arising. As a client, you want to ensure you are familiar with the progress of the consultant's efforts throughout. Should it become necessary to halt the project mid-stream, or to take a different approach either within the project or at the conclusion of the project to accomplish the intended goals, you should require status reports. This also protects you from the consultant claiming at the last moment that the project is much bigger than either of you realized and that it can be completed correctly only if the scope of it is expanded or the relationship is extended.

Scheduling Meetings

Scheduling meetings with a resource that does not work directly for you or for your company internally presents challenges for many clients. As the manager of an internal employee, you can mandate attendance at a meeting. In most cases with an external resource, you have to align calendars to accomplish what you wish in a meeting. While you can threaten, cajole, or intimidate the consultant upon occasion with the future business potential as the bait, in the final analysis, the consultant is not employed directly by you and, therefore, is less likely to be cowered into a meeting time. Having said that, there are few consultants who will not make every effort to accommodate their clients' schedules where possible. After all, it is meeting clients' needs and being perceived as easy to do business with that most consultants use as their differentiation point from other consultants. As you approach the final phases of a project, be sure to conclude any meetings that are needed prior to the final deliverable being completed.

As a personal aside, I was once scheduled to "roll out" training to a client's national sales forces across five regions in successive weeks. The client had to delay the schedule because I could not get final sign off on the course content to be included in the participant manual. All the work had been done on my end, but the client was unable to get the committee together to approve the manual, so the training was delayed for over a month until we could get it done. In that instance, there were no changes made to the materials, and although I had offered to e-mail them the files, no one was eager to study it on their own. They wanted the security of making a group decision without having to assume responsibility for their decision. Nevertheless, the project was delayed until all the members of the training committee could meet.

Final Payment

Lastly, I want to share something that I have experienced lately as projects come to conclusions. With the economy being less vibrant than it was a few years ago, more clients are looking to stretch their payments to outside vendors to longer terms. Many consultants send invoices that state they are to be paid upon receipt of the invoice, and many clients routinely ignore that and pay on their preferred payment cycles. The consultant is caught in a vise: If the consultant squeaks about it, the fear is the client will sever the relationship and seek other consulting support. On the other hand, if a consultant's cash flow is not well managed, the consultancy might fail. The failure will not be because of lack of sales, nor will it be due to poor management of expenses. Rather, it is a function of not having the funds on hand when they are needed to pay expenses. It is for this reason that consultants depend on clients to pay their invoices on a timely basis.

I had occasion a few years back to work with a major beverage company as a consultant. We had signed a multi-project contract with payments to follow upon completion of each of a series of discrete events. At the conclusion of each of those, I submitted an invoice for that event's completion. The client began to fall behind on payments, but I continued to move forward with the subsequent phases of the project (you might take me to task for that, but I assumed that the payments would catch up with the work at some point). The project began in April, and by August, we still had not been paid for the April work, and each subsequent month's invoices. I placed a call to my client contact and inquired about the lack of payment and wanted to ensure that the invoices had been received, they were correctly completed, and there was no issue with anything I had submitted (thereby alerting the client that if I was not the hold-up on payment, by process of elimination, they had to be the reason I was not being paid on a timely basis). The client gave me a hundred and one excuses over the next three months as to why I had not been paid (and with each month, I was completing additional work and submitting additional invoices). Finally, with exasperation, the client angrily lashed out at me and exclaimed that they were having a bad year, so they were going to hold onto all my invoices and pay the total out of the following year's budget. Had they told me that up front, I would have likely agreed to it and made other arrangements for the short-term cash flow needs. But given how devious they attempted to be with avoiding the issue, I explained that their shortfall is not my concern and that I had performed faithfully to the agreement we had struck and, therefore, was entitled to remuneration. The long and short of it is that I no longer include them among my client roster (and they no longer have me on their preferred vendor list), but I have told this story to every person I can to try to rally other vendors from working for them and have endeavored to work with their competitors to bury them as best as I can.

I cannot tell you if my efforts are successful in reducing their market position or share, but this former client shall not have the benefit of my counsel or expertise at any time in my life. Consultants will very often bend over backwards to keep and maintain cordial relationships with clients, but if a client abuses the consultant, it is the rare consultant who will accept it meekly and not seek retribution. It all comes down to treating others as you wish to be treated. The consultant has bills to pay just like you do as a client. How would you feel if your paycheck was withheld due to circumstances beyond your control? Not many readers of this book would like going a day, never mind weeks or months, without payment for work provided.

References

The consultant might ask for references upon the completion of a project. The consultant is mindful that the best-selling approach of his or her services is word of mouth and an endorsement from a client, and especially a client that is seen as being a market leader. Therefore, the consultant might request permission to include you as a reference for prospects to contact to confirm project skills, relationship strengths, etc. To the extent that you are comfortable doing that for the consultant and are pleased with the work done, it is a nice gesture (even one that you can suggest to the consultant). If you are not pleased with the work done, it is appropriate to decline the invitation to do so. Should someone ask a direct question of the consultant's abilities, always answer honestly, however, do not volunteer to besmirch the consultant's work. Trying to barter a preferred fee from the consultant in exchange for a recommendation upon completion of the project I think is ethically gray, but I certainly understand how that could be done so that both parties benefit.

Internal/External References

References can either be sought for within the same company or for opportunities outside the company. A reference within the same company as the client contact might simply be an introduction or a passed-along e-mail or voice mail to the new potential client contact. A reference outside the company might take many forms:

- A quote from the client contact that appears on consultant's printed brochures or other marketing collateral materials to be distributed to prospects
- A Web site presence through links or examples of prior work
- Joint presentations at industry conferences (thereby giving an endorsement of the consultant's approach, methods, and abilities)
- An agreement to field phone calls or other contacts from prospects and to share with the prospect your experience with the consultant

Regardless of the reference being provided, be sure to put the parameters around it that you are comfortable with. For example, you will field no more than three phone calls within a two-month period, or you will present at a single conference of the consultant's choosing and he or she will need to do all of the logistical work to set up the speaking engagement. Failure to do so can lead to hard feelings and misaligned expectations. Clarify your level of commitment and then stick to it.

Assess Success of Engagement

Of all the steps and procedures relevant to exiting the consulting relationship, the one that is probably done least often—and when it is done, it is not done particularly effectively—is the assessment of the engagement from the perspective of how to improve upon it in the future. Regardless of whether you, as the client, choose to use the same consultant in the future or not, there should still be a review of the project as a post-mortem effort. All too often, the crisis of the moment in corporate life pre-empts the employees' ability to analyze what transpired and apply the wisdom to future projects. In an effort to address the latest task assigned to them, the last task is merely treated as a box on their "to-do list" to be checked off as having been completed and then filed or forgotten.

Lessons Learned

As the Spanish philosopher Santayana taught, if we choose not to learn from the past, we are destined to repeat it. And so, the vicious cycle of poorly executed projects, horribly managed assignments, and lackluster results continue without cessation. Rather than promulgate the continuation of this into the future, the wise client manager would create a debrief session to truly study what went well, what was less successful, and equally as important, what would need to be done in the future to anticipate the problems that did arise and address them, or at least minimize them.

Modifications

The most effective example of modifications being made as the result of a post-mortem meeting that I was ever involved in was with the Nabisco Company. A few years back, they were introducing a software-based tool to provide their sales force with insights on their business and their customers' business (retailer) so that product pricing, assortment, and shelving decisions could be done more effectively. The project was complex, requiring multiple vendors to coordinate efforts, and the deadlines were immovable, so everything had to occur on time, or the entire effort was going to fail. After many long nights, false starts, and software and hardware calamities, the project was successfully launched. Rather than sit back and celebrate though, the Nabisco team and the key vendors were required to attend and participate in one last meeting to review the project and any "lessons learned." In the most frank and candid discussion format, Nabisco employees and the vendors dissected the project, not with an eye toward blaming or holding people accountable for failure, but with an eye toward improving:

- Communication among the project team (both within Nabisco and across vendors)
- Quality control standards
- Project management
- Documentation and support
- Role assignments and performance expectations

Coming out of that meeting, a series of modifications in their approach to large-scale endeavors were drafted that this particular division of Nabisco was going to incorporate into all future consulting projects of a similar magnitude and level of complexity. After that experience, I had my eyes opened as to what it *should* be like and have worked to include a similar experience with all my subsequent clients.

Public Relations

There is a synergistic benefit to the public relations efforts that both the consultant and the client can choose to pursue on the heels of a successful project. As mentioned before, some clients will be asked by the consultant to participate in industry forums extolling the virtues of a particular process, approach taken, or other consultant-provided service. The client benefits from this exchange by claiming to be, or reinforcing their position as, a progressive company or leading-edge practitioner in the industry. This is helpful in:

- Recruiting new hires
- Attracting better deals or terms from suppliers interested in working with an industry leader and growing their business with the recognized leader
- Boosting morale internally as employees take greater pride in being rewarded for their efforts and receiving accolades or industry recognition

The consultant benefits from this exchange through:

- Being aligned with the industry leader and being credited with participating in the success (and therefore, suggesting that the same or similar results can be acquired if another company were to hire the consultant to "do that for us")

- Name recognition within the industry
- Public forum opportunities to discuss (and brag about) how the project was acquired, any facets within the project completion that are of interest or unique, etc.

Of course, there has to be a mutual agreement from both parties that they want to participate in public relations efforts. This is not always the case. Some of the reasons why clients have told me that they do not wish to participate in these efforts include:

- Confidential or proprietary nature of the project
- Unwillingness to share with competitors the company's strategic or tactical advantage
- Corporate policy to limit those who are authorized to present or speak on behalf of the company to a few executives to ensure that nothing is said or done that might be different than the cor- porate-preferred message
- Fear that the project will be less successful over time, and so they do not wish to go on record touting their success and ultimately have to retract or minimize their promotion of the project as a success

The range of public relations efforts differ, and some clients are will- ing to do one, but not another. The most common avenues for public relations activities are:

1. **Articles.** The client either authors or co-authors articles for industry publications, general press, or other journals that include mention of the project. Most often, the project is used as an example of how the company or the industry is addressing a vex- ing issue that confronts many companies, or how the company is meeting consumer needs. The article has to have the reader's interest in mind, and if it comes off too much like a "commercial" for the project, for the company, or for the consultant, the editor will likely reject it.

2. **Quotes in article.** Some consultants/clients are uncomfortable or unwilling to write an article, but are very happy to provide quotes

or to talk about the project with a journalist writing a story about the project. This provides a "third-party endorsement" from a trusted or recognized objective source, and the reader is likely to give more credence and credibility to this account than if someone touts their own strengths.

3. **Presentations at industry conferences.** Here again, the approach must focus on the conference attendees' interest in the project as something they might want to do to address the issue confronted, or in some other way appeal to the attendees as something worthwhile to listen to and incorporate into their business decisions.

4. **Advertising.** While not typically thought of as "public relations," an advertisement that extols the virtues of a project's impact on the company's ability to meet their needs that also mentions the affiliation with the consultant hired to assist the company does perform the same or similar function of endorsement (though it is not "third party").

Pros and Cons of Advertisements

Let's look at the positives and negatives of agreeing to do an advertisement at the conclusion of the project.

On the positive side, if the project addresses a need that positions the company to be more competitive and responsive, or in some other way provides a "good story" to tell customers, suppliers, or others, then it might make sense to use the project as an element or focus of an advertising campaign. Good examples of this can be found on many airport walls where software and consulting firms are referenced in billboard-type advertisements being credited with helping their clients meet the needs of their customers through some more accurate mechanized or electronic product ordering system or distribution approach.

On the negative side, there is a perspective that "professionals" don't need to advertise and that it is unseemly. While this perception is changing, there is still a remnant that exists that would have professionals sell and market themselves through word-of-mouth alone. The thinking employed is that physicians, attorneys, accountants, and consultants who resort to advertising must be "hurting" for business or are charlatans who are not very good at what they do, and so they advertise to prey on the unsuspecting. While a pretty cynical viewpoint, there are those who will see the advertisement and might feel that way, and as a result, will view the message with a jaundiced eye.

Another negative is that a competitor can use a company's admission that they sought or used outside consultants against them. If not carefully worded and positioned, what might at first appear to be a positive statement can be turned against the company that is advertising and be made to appear to be a weakness.

Checklist for Using Consultants

1. Has a defined point or event been determined for when the relationship with the consultant will conclude?
2. Has all of the administrative, contractual, and expense or performance tracking been completed?
3. What level of commitment (if any) are you prepared to provide to leverage the project's success through advertisements, public relations campaigns, or other pursuits that are tangential to the success of the project per se, but might be strategically important to the company?

Maximizing Results

Key Learning Points:

- Assuming control for the project and avoiding dependence on the consultant
- Cooperatively sharing the success with other internal departments without damaging chances for acceptance
- Summary of consulting engagement process

Business is like a wheelbarrow—it stands still unless someone pushes it.

In choosing to work with consultants, one of the primary goals (as previously discussed) is to accomplish a task that for one reason or another is better suited to using an outside agent. However, even in this scenario, the focus on results should not be lost. The overarching purposes of the project and the consultant's use are to ensure the client's maximum benefit. The consultant is hired to achieve the project's objective, not to influence the client contact's political considerations that can drive corporate decisions toward the use of consultants. Regardless of the other benefits that the client contact might accrue for using a consultant, it still behooves the consultant and client contact to ensure that the project is completed and delivers the expected results.

Philosophically, corporate clients of mine approach their decision and the criteria employed to use consultants in general—and my services specifically—in vastly different ways. There is no one "right way" to approach the maximization of results. Each client's situation calls for a different set of metrics to evaluate the decision.

Self-Reliance or Addicted to Outsiders

Some clients want to build the competencies of their internal staffs and view the use of consultants as a temporary or "stop gap" measure to be applied until such time as *they can take it over themselves*. These clients want to be actively involved in the project, ask many questions, are quite participative, and often form project teams and require frequent interaction between the consultant and the members of the team. It is not unusual for the clients that subscribe to this approach to want to work alongside the consultant to observe, take notes, and become apprentices to the consultant for the duration of the project.

Other clients of mine much prefer to use my services and those of other consultants to fill the occasional (or even not-so occasional) needs that arise for which they do not have a resident expert, or for other strategic reasons (budgets being a major one), they determine it is better to use an outside consultant to address those needs. These clients have determined that it is more cost-effective to pay for a consultant's services that are a variable cost incurred only when there is a project to be completed that requires that consultant's expertise or level of competence, than to pay for the salary and benefits of a full-time employee dedicated to projects requiring that skill set. Rather than absorb the costs of health care, benefits, and office space, these clients would rather "turn on the spigot" when a consultant's services are needed and turn it off when business needs dictate a reduction in spending. These clients, most times, do not want to actively participate in the project's work, preferring to treat it as a commodity being purchased. Either it is not seen as something that will be necessary to understand because it is a one-time occurrence that once resolved, will not reappear, or it is not something they have a desire to understand—that is why the consultant is hired, so the client does not have to worry or devote time to addressing the issue. Similar to having your 12-year-old child program your VCR for you, once it is done, you do not have to do it again, so you probably don't care how it is accomplished.

The core argument that clients need to address is whether to hire the expertise in the form of a full-time employee (with all the so-called feeding and nurturing that goes along with that, such as career pathing, managing, and development), or to hire an outside resource for the project, with the understanding that at the conclusion of the project, or by a mutually agreed-upon decision made within the project's duration, the relationship will end. On a per-day basis, hiring an outside resource is often seen as being a more expensive option than having a full-time employee. However, what is missing from this analysis and skews it greatly is the impact of having that resource on staff full time and having to pay for that person's services whether or not they are being fully utilized. In some instances, the person can be slotted or used to accomplish other tasks, making their utility broader than just the one area of expertise. Equally as frequent, though, is the situation where a skill is required at a level of expertise that many "generalists" cannot provide, so an outside resource with that level of experience, knowledge, and competence is then hired, thus the client is "double paying" for the skill set (the employee's and the consultant's).

The third approach is a hybrid of the two above. The company perceives a recurrent need in the future for a particular strength and hires a lesser experienced person with the understanding that they will "develop" that person's strengths by pairing him or her on the first project or two with a recognized expert from a consulting firm. That consultant will essentially mentor and develop the internal resource so that in the future, the employee will be able to assume control of the project by him- or herself. The company saves a portion of the salary that would have been necessary to hire a more experienced person to handle the first few assignments, builds their own internal competence, and ensures that the first few projects done by the new employee are done correctly and that the person learns the best approaches to use from a trusted resource.

Put another way, as a client, you will be confronted with the decision to build self-reliance or to rely on the expertise of outsiders and risk the danger of the expertise and know-how leaving with the consultant upon conclusion of the project. I have seen many clients become addicted to using outsiders and skip over their own resources for projects that could have been handled by internal employees. The reason for passing over internal resources and hiring a consultant is not because those employees could have been applied to more strategic projects that had to be completed concurrently with the project being outsourced, but rather because there is a perceived air of sophistication or complexity lent to the project by virtue of it being assigned to the consultant. But when these projects conclude, and the consultant leaves the company's employ, there is no one left within the company who knows how to implement or continue to manage the project in the consultant's absence and one of two things typically occur:

1. The project is abandoned and any and all benefits from it are lost due to neglect or improper management.
2. The consultant is urgently called back to resuscitate a dying project (and thereby ensures a nice payday for the foreseeable future).

A project is doomed to fail if it does not either integrally include an internal resource as part of the project, enabling that person to assume leadership of the project, or at the absolute minimum, include implementation or integration steps as provided by the consultant to be employed upon completion of the consulting project.

Corporate Philosophy

Forming the strategic approach to deciding whether to hire a full-time employee or a consultant is usually based on the general corporate culture and philosophy toward the business. The following questions must be considered when making this decision:

• Does the business tend to be very short-term focused and prefer to manage against the "here and now" kind of objectives? If so, a consultant might be called to address an immediate project that has a tight deadline.

- Is there a pervasive feeling that employees perform their best when under the pressure of a crisis or tight deadline, and when the "chips are down, we throw resources at a problem and all help out"? Again, this is a scenario where a consultant might be part of the "mix" of resources tossed at a project, or it might be a situation where a consultant would not be used since the company prefers to use internal resources and swarm the project with sheer quantity of resources. In this situation, a crisis often occurs shortly after, and the consultant is then hired with little time to perform as the project flounders or is poorly managed.

- Is the organization generally flexible and does it accommodate the development of resources in a managed, yet specific-to-the-situation basis? (If so, the company might put a premium on developing resources and, therefore, will give employees time to work through issues and avoid having to use a consultant. Conversely, as mentioned before, it is also an ideal time to bring in a consultant and have that expert teach the employee how to perform the project and ensure that there are no bad habits developed or missteps taken.

- Is the organization more hierarchically driven and employees are expected to perform the tasks they are assigned, but projects outside that sphere of expertise or even on the periphery of that competence are farmed out to other resources more expert than that of internal employees?

- Lastly, is the organization one that prides itself on being entrepreneurial and, therefore, feels comfortable "throwing smart people at problems and allowing them to develop solutions as they see fit"? If the company is entrepreneurial in spirit, it will often be so busy growing, that it does not stop to see the commonalities among business problems—lack of process, little focus on execution, few systems in place to track, modify, evaluate, etc. While the pressure cooker of having to get it done can generate viable solutions to business opportunities, it can also result in lots of frustration that could have been avoided with a properly managed consulting project.

Anecdotally, I have two stories related to this concept. On one occasion in my career, I worked as an internal employee for a hierarchically driven firm and had the following occur:

I was passed over for an assignment that required the development of a sales competency matrix to evaluate and then rank each of over 100 salespeople in the company. My management determined that this project would have exceeded my capabilities and outsourced it to an external consultant with a brochure that included a bullet on sales assessments as a core strength of the consultancy. The consultant immediately wanted my input and perspective on how to approach the project (under the guise of better understanding the points of view currently being expressed by internal resources, and not as a way of figuring out how to deliver what was soon to be recognized as a task well beyond the capabilities of this consultant). The project was completed and did achieve what it was designed to do, but management never knew that it was an internal employee who was driving the project and all the important factors and criteria. That consultant did eventually pay me back for the assistance some years later. That payback indirectly led to the next anecdote.

A fairly entrepreneurial firm that prided itself on hiring good people and asked them to stretch themselves to achieve even greater outputs than they would have believed possible employed me for a number of years as an internal employee. New management assumed control and decided that it was more advantageous to close down certain functions and divisions of the company and save the cost of the resource. What management then decided to do was to outsource those same functions to external providers. Coincidentally, one of those providers of services turned out to be me. So, the company had me as an internal resource and essentially was getting the benefit of my services as part of my employment, but then chose to contract with me directly as an outside resource to achieve the same outcome. This model of outsourcing happens quite frequently and many companies benefit by ensuring that they are getting resources who know the company and are familiar with policies and procedures. Consultants have a much quicker learning curve this way, too: They are working with people they know, and for a company and product they are intimately familiar.

As a client, the biggest caveat to follow is to prevent yourself from being shortsighted to the point of missing opportunities because you are swayed by "that is how we do things around here." Think strategically about how you wish to use your internal resources, and what projects should be completed by outside resources. When making the decision to use outside resources, give consideration to whether it is in your individual/department/company's best interest to assign an internal resource to shadow or follow the consultant and learn how the project is to be completed. Or is this project so unique and unlikely to need to be addressed again that it would be a colossal waste of resources to learn how to do something that will not need to be repeated?

Even if the project is not one that will likely ever need to be addressed again, the same guidance that is offered for projects that are more commonly completed applies: Be sure that you or someone you trust is aware of how to best implement and integrate any solutions that the consultant provides or suggests.

Reinvent the Wheel or Spread the Gospel

As mentioned throughout this book, the decision to alert other functions, departments, or executives of the use of a consultant is one that should be made with plenty of forethought. The repercussions of not handling this awareness building (positively or negatively) can echo through the life of the project and can either facilitate success or hamper the ensuing progress made on the project. The ramifications of including/not including others in the work of the consultant will remain long after the official conclusion of the project.

Obviously, if the project is impacting all functions directly (such as Y2K or other enterprise-wide computer issues, customer relationship management processes, or a new organizational structure project), the better the project team communicates to the rest of the organization, the more likely it is that the intervention will be successful. In projects that are more focused on one aspect of the company (review of a department's managers' skills, improving manufacturing or operational efficiencies, or integrating software for the accounts payable function that is non-accessible by other departments), it might not be relevant or necessary to bring others into the discussion or execution of the project.

One of the strong determinants of a consulting project's maximization of results is how well the project team handles this aspect of the assignment. In some instances, you might direct the team to *not* share details of the project with others. Reasons for this might be:

- The project is confidential in nature and it would be strategically disadvantageous to allow the information to get into competitors' hands. By keeping a tight rein on who has access to the information, you minimize the opportunity for "loose lips to sink ships." However, this approach does breed rumor and cynicism among fellow employees not included in the project. In the absence of information, people will create their own realities, small snippets of information (sometimes misinformation) will spontaneously emerge, and the reaction of others within your company might serve to create unintended problems that will need to be addressed. Therefore, use this more secretive approach *only* when you *can* control access to information, it is essential that access be controlled, and the absence of more open communication is of such strategic importance, that it is worth the potential downside of having to deal with rumors, innuendos, and misinformation.
- The project is sensitive in nature (downsizing, search for new CEO, new product launches, selling off of a division, etc.), and the company is still exploring options and does not want to set off mass hysteria or create a distraction for employees. In this instance, the project team might prefer to not be very communicative with others within the company. If the project is that sensitive in nature, chances are that it cannot include the input of other company employees outside the project team through its completion. Should the expertise of others (within the company, or external to the company, such as customers, suppliers, industry observers) be warranted, the secrecy is broken. In the event that the project team tries to anticipate the likely reaction of others and provides a fake reason for the need for the insights requested (or gives the project a "code name" to give it some secret agent panache), the truth will often be sniffed out, and management will no longer be trusted should they ever ask for

input again from the company employees or others who were "duped." While there are positive reasons for creating "code names" for projects, they should not be used to hide the true purpose of the project from those contributing.

In other instances, you might only need to communicate that a project is taking place within the company/division/function, that it is intended to accomplish "x," and that all normal business will continue as usual. Should there be disruption to the day-in and day-out business processes or results during the project, then it would be appropriate to share:

- How long the project will last
- What new or other processes will be required for business transactions during the project
- The possibility of time delays, if any, in getting the department or function to respond to requests as a result of the project
- What the expectation is in the future (how this will help, streamline, be more efficient, etc.) as a result of the project

As the rest of the organization is only tangentially involved in the project and does not have to change how they interact (or has to modify their actions only for the duration of the project), simple communication with the rest of the organization might suffice without any further need for involvement of others.

Communication within the Company

Lastly—and frankly the way *most* projects in my consulting career *should* be handled, but are not necessarily handled—communicate with the organization what the intent of the project is, how it will impact the organization globally or generally, and how it will affect effectiveness in working with other departments or functions. Not stopping there, the project team should also solicit the insights of other departments to see if their perspective(s) on how the function or department embarking on the project can improve. There is tremendous power in asking others for their help:

- We all want to be perceived as being helpful, and if someone asks for our advice on how to improve, very few of us would not welcome the chance to help.
- It prevents or at least minimizes the opportunity for others to purposely prevent the project from succeeding. It would be highly unusual for someone or some department to refuse to offer assistance or to offer poor counsel in attempt to "one up" the requesting department.
- It improves the communication between the departments. Now processes can be explained, and answers can be offered to the question, "Why do you do it that way?" It also allows the department using the consultant to inquire if there are changes the department offering assistance could make to improve how they interact with the first department.
- It involves the other departments in the planning, execution, or implementation of the project. In so doing, it removes any of the secretiveness of the project and prevents misunderstandings or rumors from developing.
- It reinforces that the company is acting in a cooperative and cohesive fashion and not allowing itself to get caught up in political infighting or gamesmanship.

Many of the training projects I am hired to complete are initially scoped by the client as being department or function specific. Often, after discussions with the client contact, the project evolves into one that either includes members of other departments in the training itself (with the strong benefit of bringing people together who ordinarily work off of assumptions about the other, but without any real exposure on which to base those assumptions), or includes the insights of the other functions in building the objectives or skills necessary to be trained, including those skills that are germane to interacting more effectively with the other functions in order to more effectively do the job.

Previously in this book, we touched upon how consultants are often treated as property of the initial client contact who hired the consultant. While this is clearly not to anyone's benefit long term (or in most instances, short term either), this does raise a point that deserves mention and further elucidation. The point is whether the original client contact has a responsibility back to the organization to share that consultant's strengths or ideas in areas that do not directly impact that client contact's sphere of influence or are outside the span of control of that manager.

As a consultant, it is imperative that new business opportunities be constantly sourced. The most fertile ground to do that is the existing client (for all the previously referenced reasons). However, the question remains, should the project manager be the one obligated to introduce the consultant to others within the organization that can use the services of the consultant? Put another way, is it better to allow each function to "reinvent the wheel" each time a similar issue arises within the company (without being aware that it was solved elsewhere within the company)? When seen that way, few readers will agree that in this instance, every department or function should react independently of the total organization. Yet, we can all cite examples of one function either choosing not to communicate their successes with the rest of the organization (and the subsequent need to re-learn in one area of the company what has already been learned elsewhere in the company), or the refusal to accept that what might have worked in one area of the company could possibly work in some other area of the company.

NIMBY/NCH

The challenge is how to best spread the "gospel" of successful projects without lauding individual or personal successes over other departments or functions, and at the same time, providing them with access to the consultant, the project, or the methodologies employed. One very successful technique that I have encountered is to publicly thank the other departments for their contribution to the project work in an e-mail and copy the consultant in the letter (thereby providing access to the consultant for any other executives interested in contracting for similar projects). Of course, the informal network always works well (lunch conversations, hallway asides, etc.).

One of the hurdles that my business has had to overcome in working with multi-national companies, or even multi-division companies, is how to penetrate these other entities and not be seen as an interloper from "the other country/division." Many of us have a defense mechanism firmly in place that prevents us from seeing situations in an honest and forthright manner. Whether working in the wine and spirits industry, for a frozen food company, or with a company that delivers its product directly to the store, bypassing any need to warehouse and ship product on an "as-needed" basis, Clow Zahn Associates, LLC, has been confronted by the following initials: NIMBY and NCH.

The NIMBY, or Not In My Backyard, constituencies believe that it might be well and good for some "other" group or division within the firm to require or even solicit the assistance of a consultant, but consulting is not something that is required nor even requested in "this" division. Even when others within the company can clearly see the benefit of the consulting project recently completed being applied to the sister division or a functional equivalent in another country, the local management might turn a blind eye to it. The best approach that we have been able to take with these managers is to engage them in a discussion where possible and get them to express *their* ideas of what is necessary to improve their function's performance. Once it is not seen as something being foisted upon them, the receptivity to the idea usually heightens. Rather than focus them on the negative connotation of "needing" help, the conversation is focused on the positive of how to better achieve what they are striving to accomplish.

The cousins of the NIMBY group are the NCH folks, or the Not Created Here flock. These people hold fast to the idea that they have a monopoly on all good thinking and that any ideas that were not hatched and nurtured within the confines of their surroundings cannot possibly be meritorious. We have seen this perception applied commonly when attempting to take a consulting project across geographical borders. Now, to be sure, there are differences in how business is conducted and how managers behave in different countries. However, once noted and accommodated for, many projects are as easily transferable across country lines as they are across state lines in the United States. Even language concerns and the need for translation services can be accounted for (where necessary) and overcome so as not to prevent a consulting project from achieving its intended outcome. Here again, the easiest way to convert them is to meet or talk with them and get them to elucidate their new vision or reality of what *should* be done and then work with them to achieve it. Most of the time, that vision will closely resemble the success of the previously completed project.

Book Summary/Checklist for Working with a Consultant

To truly maximize the impact of the consultant's work, you will need to reassess the following criteria:

- Have you given thought to why you are using a consultant? Are the reasons beneficial to the organization, or are they selfishly motivated?
- Have you decided on what criteria to use to select the consultant? If you are unsure of how you will assess the consultant, or if your criteria are not aligned with the reasons for selecting the consultant in the prior step, you might want to reconsider how you will judge the success of the project. To maximize the success of the project, you will need to first identify what success will look like, and then choose your consultant based on that consultant being able to provide proof of their ability to assist you and your organization in achieving that outcome.
- Once the consultant has been selected, have the specific contractual terms been spelled out and agreed upon so that there is clarity on what is expected (either results and/or process to achieve those results)? Even well-intentioned and honest consultants and clients should document what their agreement is between them to ensure that there is no confusion or misunderstanding. A contract is not an admission that you do not trust the other, and it is not a prelude to a planned lawsuit. It is a measured and calculated step to communicate what each party is willing to commit to the completion of the project and what expectations have been established and agreed upon. To maximize results in working with consultants, this document and the process required to complete it drive the necessary communication between client and consultant to ensure that both parties are in alignment with each other and understand the requirements of the project.
- Have you chosen and communicated how you will manage the project? Will the work be custom developed or more syndicated?

Will a committee manage the project? Who will have final say? Who will be involved in the day-to-day administration of the contractual obligations? There should be no surprises between consultant and client when it comes to how the project will be managed and what level of involvement will be required from each of the parties.

- Have the working relationship and associated dynamics been addressed? Who "speaks" for the client company? Who "speaks" for the consultant? Will there be a need for written reports and recaps? Will there be frequent need for status meetings, or will the project be completed without that requirement? Will the work be done on-site or will the consultant complete the project at their location?

- Have the criteria for evaluating the performance of the consultant been established and communicated? Are there standards of acceptable performance or expected results in place? Do the criteria and standards support the intended goal of the project, or are they at odds with the intended purpose of the project?

- Is there a strategy in place for the continuation of the project, reinforcement of the new skills provided, and maintenance of the delivered product upon the conclusion of the project? Too many projects fail as a result of the consultant leaving the client's employ and there not being any plan in place to assume control for the project within the client organization. What the consultant leaves in his or her wake is a legacy of high performance that is viewed as a failure or just not practical because there was no one around to assume responsibility for the project on an ongoing basis.

List of Consulting Firms

A list of some of the largest consulting firms in the United States is provided below. I provide this list without endorsement of any of them and do not intend to have the reader think that these are recommended, or that by virtue of not being listed below, that the consulting organization is to be avoided or is not worthy of use. I provide this list just as a way to give the reader access to some of the names of consulting firms that are commonly used by major businesses.

A.T. Kearney – www.atkearney.com
Bain & Company – www.bain.com
BearingPoint – www.bearingpoint.com
Booz Allen Hamilton – www.bah.com
Boston Consulting Group – www.bcg.com
Cambridge Technology Partners – www.novell.com/ctp
Cap Gemini Ernst & Young – www.cgey.com
Clow Zahn Associates, LLC – www.clowzahn.com
Deloitte Consulting – www.dc.com
DiamondCluster International – www.diamondcluster.com
Hewitt Associates – www.hewitt.com

IBM Global Services – www.ibm.com
Kurt Salmon Associates – www.kurtsalmon.com
McKinsey & Company – www.mckinsey.com
Mercer Management Consulting – www.mercermc.com
Monitor Group – www.monitor.com
PriceWaterhouseCoopers Management Consulting Services –
    www.pwcglobal.com
Sapient Corporation – www.sapient.com
Razorfish – www.razorfish.com
Towers Perrin – www.towers.com
Watson Wyatt Worldwide – www.watsonwyatt.com

Sample Proposal and Contract

On the following pages is a sample proposal and contractual agreement used to detail how my firm would approach a client's training need. I have removed any identifying information about the client from this proposal so that you can focus on the format of the proposal. This is just one example of a proposal, as there is no industry standard or approved template for consulting projects. By and large, the proposal and agreement/contract are formalities that document what has already been covered verbally or in previous communications between you and the consultant. The proposal is ideally not the time for you to learn about pricing or approach. The exception to this is when you are using an approach to minimize advantages given to one consulting organization over another through a Request For Proposal (RFP) process. In that instance, you might publish or distribute your desire for consultants to provide you with how they would approach a particular opportunity and what the costs would be associated with that approach. Then, each consultant is expected to put their best offer on the table to win the business.

CLIENT COMPANY NAME
Revised Proposal
"Best Practices" and Fundamentals of Negotiation Workshops
September 12, 2000

Clow Zahn Associates, LLC
Westport, CT 06880

September 12, 2000

Mr. Client Contact
Senior Vice President, Sales & Marketing
Company Name
Street Address
City, State, Zip Code

Dear Client Contact:

I am glad we got to speak yesterday (Monday the 11th of September) and further clarify what your vision is for the proposed "Best Practices" Workshop for your internal sales support group. Given that you have received a prior proposal from Clow Zahn Associates, LLC on this project, and I do not wish to confuse the issue by having two proposals for the same project, this agreement shall replace the prior proposal sent as it now reflects a better understanding of how we can best meet your training objectives.

We appreciate your thinking of us to assist you in realizing your vision for transitioning the Client Company sales and marketing efforts toward a more "Business Management" focus, and believe there are synergies to be gained by using us for both the "Best Practices" workshop, and the more standard/traditional Introduction to Negotiation Skills workshop scheduled for first quarter of 2001. Clow Zahn Associates, LLC (CZA) has assisted other companies in making a similar transition, and we feel that our prior experience would nicely complement your initiative and goal of more effectively practicing "Best Practices" in the unique market in which you compete.

As the industry continues to undergo rapid change, there is an increasing need for improving upon previous results—often without additional resources. It is therefore incumbent upon manufacturers to critically assess their "go to market" strategies and application of "Best Practices" with the perspective of ensuring an adequate "return" on monies spent to "build the business." As a result of our discussions, and our prior experience within the industry, CZA has been asked to confirm our mutual understanding of the agreement to move jointly ahead on this initiative.

Background

Client Company is the world's largest specialist in the production and marketing of "x," "y," and "z," and allied products and services. While best known for <particular distribution channel products>, they also produce a wide range of specialty products and services for other applications, including the <list of other channels and sectors>. With distribution in channels as diverse as supermarkets, after market auto supplies stores, do it yourself (DIY) trade classes, mass merchandisers, specialty retailers, etc., Client Company's presence is universal in outlets selling these products.

While clearly a leader in the categories in which they compete, the environment in which they sell is evolving and changing away from a manufacturer-dominated forum toward a more "fact-based," retailer-driven approach that is dependent upon the precepts of "Best Practices."

Therefore, management has determined that to more effectively maintain the dominance in the category and meet the needs of the changing landscape of the industry "head-on," the enhancement of the sales force's skills in "Best Practices" is a required step to be undertaken.

To leverage the burgeoning emphasis on "Best Practices" within both the less sophisticated <name of channel> aftermarket industry at large, and the larger, more progressive retailers, as well as within Client Company specifically, demands a thorough understanding of the impact of promotional decisions on brand; category; inventory management strategies, shelf placement, and merchandising; customer and consumer penetration; and a deeper understanding of how "Best Practices" is applied by retailers. Given the dearth of syndicated data in many instances, the approaches used to practice "Best Practices" need to be applicable for both data-rich environments and those that are bereft of POS data.

Because of our experience with other companies in similar situations, CZA has prepared a proposal outlining how we would work with you to develop and deliver both a **Client Company Best Practices** and a **Fundamentals of Negotiation Workshop.**

Objective

If the situation described above is accurate, then we believe the objective of this project should be twofold:

I. Develop, design, and deliver a one and one-half day Client Company–Name-Specific "Best Practices" Workshop that will establish the skills and knowledge within the sales support organization necessary to maximize the effectiveness of industry best practices.

II. Deliver a Fundamentals of Negotiation Workshop to build awareness of concepts, terminology, and practices for the sales force to be delivered in Q1 of 2001.

Approach

Given these objectives, CZA will work with Client Company to create the "Best Practices Workshop" (a one and one-half day workshop) that addresses the following (data allowing):

- *Brief* introduction to the trends that led to the evolution of "Best Practices" (including, but not limited to acquisition/consolidations, channel-blurring, e-options, changing consumer needs)
- Best practices—consumer facts
  - Purchase dynamics (either conceptual if not available to us, or client specific if provided)
  - Demographics and how they are used for micro-marketing (selecting clusters, determining specific actions to take with a cluster, etc.)
  - Spectra analysis (if available to compare Client consumer to retailer's target consumer)
- Best practices—promotion
  - Incremental volume discussion (what it is, how it differs from promoted volume, etc.)
  - Promotion evaluation (volume, pricing, duration, coverage/ACV, and effect/lift)
  - Comparison/contrasts with category average, competitive brand impacts, retailer effects, and other influencers on promotional performance
- Best practices—pricing
  - Explanation of base price, promoted, and average price
  - Explanation of indices and how to use in relation to volume projections
  - Price elasticity discussion
- Best practices—assortment
  - Possible discussion of panel, profitability, and volumetric influences (TBD in conjunction with Client Company management)
- Best practices—opportunity identification
  - Fair share (promoted vs. base)
  - Sales rate comparisons
  - Brand share comparisons
  - Out of stocks (OOS)
  - Full distribution/open voids/substitution/projected "what-if" scenarios for new item/new distribution

- Best practices calculations (not as a separate module necessarily, but to be embedded in the appropriate module above, and maybe to be collected in an appendix for easier reference)
- Promotion efficiency (including promotion volume)
- Correlation coefficients (if store level data is available)
- Power sorts for assortment
- Assortment measures (sales/item, sales rate/item, share of sales/share of items)
- Next wave of best practices—The future
- Frequency/loyalty shopper initiatives
- Total-store marketing
- Event marketing
- Portfolio management (looking at the breadth and depth of manufacturer offerings or broker's offerings and putting a strategic plan in place that encompasses many of the above facets)

The workshop will be delivered for up to 15 attendees, and CZA will provide two facilitators for the duration of the class to provide differing perspectives and provide a more engaging and interactive approach. Additionally, a master copy of all workshop materials and content will be provided to Client Company so that each attendee may be provided with a binder of the training session for future reference.

The one and one-half day Negotiation Fundamentals Workshop will cover the following topics:

- Introduction to the concepts of negotiation (what it is/is not)
- Review of the changing retail environment and landscape
- Overview of common negotiating situations Client Company confronts
- Explanation of roles of manufacturer-retailer-consumer in negotiation
- Application of the 8-step process
- Examples of "best-in-class" manufacturer outputs and retailer expectations

Qualifications

CZA is qualified to handle this project for the following reasons:

1. CZA is a targeted and specialty sales training and consulting firm.

CZA differs from large strategic consulting firms that neither focus on sales issues nor the consumer products sector. CZA concentrates in the consumer products industry and specializes in sales and related functions, i.e., broker management, team selling, business planning, sales presentation development, various analytic skills workshops (promotion, new item introduction, pricing, etc.), negotiation, category management (business process, specific tactics, integration of sales tools, etc.).

As a result of CZA's unique structure and focus, our consultants clearly understand the issues you face, are familiar with solutions that work, and are able to help you implement CZA's recommendations.

2. **CZA has extensive experience in developing, designing, and delivering tailored training curricula.**

   Jeff Clow and David Zahn have trained over 3,000 salepeople over the last 10 years and have been at the forefront in facilitating client-specific workshops that raise the expertise level of existing consumer-products manufacturers' sales forces.

3. **CZA has experience in a variety of trade classes and sales systems.**

   In completing projects, we have worked in virtually all major consumer products trade classes and with a variety of sales and marketing systems. Our experience includes:

Trade Classes:

- Food stores
- Drug stores
- Convenience stores
- Mass merchandisers
- Food service accounts
- Warehouse and club stores
- Specialty retailers (category killers, emerging classes of trade, etc.)
- Bookstores
- Department stores

Types of Sales and Distribution Systems:

- Direct store delivery systems
- Specialty products distributors (meat, beef, candy, and tobacco)
- Food service
- Direct sales forces

- Food brokers (retail, military, and food service)
- Retail merchandising services

4. **All projects are staffed with CZA Partners.**

   All of CZA's project work is completed by one of the partners/owners who have line sales and/or marketing management experience with major consumer-products companies. CZA projects are never delegated to lower-level assistants. Project work is easily implemented and integrated into your company. CZA's focus is on meeting your needs and not in building project scopes or theoretical reports.

5. **CZA utilizes a team approach.**

   The team assigned to your project will possess unique skills and experiences that fit your company's specific needs. Within CZA, Jeff Clow possesses a unique background that encompasses 25 years of sales, sales management, training, and customer management. David Zahn's background includes a degree in Instructional Design and over 12 years of professional consulting experience. By relying on a team approach, you will receive our best thinking. Additionally, our consultants regularly meet with other people in the firm to obtain additional thoughts and insights relative to your specific situation.

6. **CZA has extensive experience with other major consumer-products companies.**

   Our consultants have worked on projects for over 75 clients, and 42 of the top 50 CPG firms.

Staffing

This project will be co-managed by Jeff Clow and David Zahn. Additionally, for this program to be successfully implemented, it might require a dedicated resource within Client Company to provide access to decision makers, policies, forms, reports, or other pertinent data.

Fees

CZA is able to extend a bundled pricing of <$ amount> to Client Company based on the following:

- Up to five (5) days of meeting/consultation and/or customization to create the "Best Practices" Workshop, working in tandem with Client Company

subject-matter experts to tailor the program to meet Client Company's requirements for category and channel specificity.
- Up to 15 participants in attendance at the "Best Practices" Workshop and up to 20 participants at the Negotiation Fundamentals Workshop.
- Any additional participants beyond the above will be charged at a fee of $750 per participant.
- Client Company will retain responsibility for any incidental travel, project costs (including courier, manual copying/reproducing, and postage) associated with this project.

Fee Schedule

The payment schedule is defined below:

Activity	Fee	Timing
Signed contract	<$ amount>	Upon signature
Execution of each session	<$ amount>	At conclusion of workshops

Summary

Client Contact, we are delighted that Client Company is considering CZA for this important project. Our qualifications in the consumer products industry and our complementary strengths make us unique. Needless to say, we would be delighted to work with you and believe we can do an excellent job on this initiative.

To retain us for this assignment, please sign and date the attached agreement and return to my attention at Clow Zahn Associates, LLC, 191 Post Road W., Westport, CT 06880.

I look forward to working with you on this project.

Sincerely,

David Zahn
Managing Partner
Clow Zahn Associates, LLC

Mr. Client Contact
Senior Vice President, Sales and Marketing
Client Company Name
Street Address
City, State, Zip Code

Subject: Client Company "Best Practices" and Fundamentals of Negotiation Workshops

AGREEMENT BETWEEN
Clow Zahn Associates, LLC
AND
Client Company
For Proposal Dated September 12, 2000

This will outline the terms of an Agreement under which **Client Company** (hereinafter called the "Client") will retain the services of Clow Zahn Associates, LLC (hereafter sometimes called "CZA").

1. Effective the day this proposal is signed by both parties, the Client will retain CZA to provide professional consulting services as generally described in CZA's proposal of **September 12, 2000**. If, subsequent to the commencement of execution of the project, the Client changes the project scope and/or approach, CZA will initially determine whether it can accept such changes. If the changes are mutually acceptable to the Client and CZA, CZA will determine required adjustments in fees to accomplish the project as modified. The Client will be notified in writing of such project scope and/or approach changes and the adjusted creative fees and billing schedule.

2. **Jeff Clow and David Zahn** will have overall management responsibility for this project

3. The creative fee for this project is anticipated to be <$ amount> based on up to 15 participants for the "Best Practices" Workshop and 20 participants for the "Fundamental" Workshop (additional participants will be charged a fee of $750 per attendee) and CZA providing a master copy of materials to Client Company for duplication and distribution to attendees. CZA will devote up to five (5) days of customization in conjunction with source materials provided by Client Company to develop the "Best Practices" Workshop. This fee will be payable as follows:

   <$ amount> with signed proposal
   <$ amount> at the conclusion of each of the workshop executions

   Payment is due upon receipt of invoice.

4. Production fees (such as external copying, special binders, tabs, slides, courier services, Federal Express charges, and telephone charges) that are incurred during the execution of this project are not included in the fee. These costs will be rebilled to Client at cost.

   Any outside services that might need to be purchased will be rebilled to the Client at cost, plus a production management fee, not to exceed 10%. No outside service costs will be incurred without the express prior approval of the Client.

5. Travel and other out-of-pocket expenses incurred by CZA personnel during the execution of the project will be rebilled to the Client at cost.

6. This Agreement contemplates a professional consulting relationship between CZA and the Client with respect to the projects assigned to CZA during the term of the Agreement. As a part of this Agreement, the Client assumes full responsibility for the results of sales programs recommended or developed by CZA if such programs are implemented by the Client or under the Client's direction and are not implemented solely by CZA.

7. CZA will treat as confidential any information obtained about the Client that the Company does not ordinarily make available to the public. This obligation shall continue beyond the life of this Agreement unless and until such information is otherwise legally in the public domain.

8. This proposal is valid for a 30-day period commencing September 12, 2000. In order to retain us for this project, simply sign both copies of this Agreement in the space designated below. Please return the blue copy of the signed Agreement to the attention of David Zahn along with a check for the initial payment.

9. Client may, by written notice, cancel this Agreement at any time. In the event of such cancellation, CZA shall bill Client for all work done prior to CZA's receipt of the Notice of Cancellation, together with the cost of all work in process or under contract that cannot be cancelled, plus a cancellation fee of 10% of the unbilled creative fee detailed in Paragraph Three.

If the foregoing reflects the entire understanding of both parties, this Agreement should be signed by the principals of both the Client and CZA, and a signed copy should be provided for the files of each party.

Client Company	Clow Zahn Associates, LLC
Signature:_____	Signature:_____
Title: _____	Title: Managing Partner
Date: _____	Date: September, 12, 2000

Please retain one copy for your records and send a signed copy to: Clow Zahn Associates, LLC, 191 Post Road W., Westport, CT 06880

References

I want to also provide you with some resources for helping you make the consulting experience more positive for you and for your company. With that in mind, I submit the list below of sources to help clarify your thinking on the entire process of hiring and using consultants.

Books

For some interesting reading on how consultants can sometimes infiltrate the thinking of management and skew how companies resolve various issues in favor of the consultant's profit and loss over their own, I recommend reading:

1. Romaine, S. (2003). *Soldier of fortune 500*. Amherst, NY: Prometheus Books.
2. Lewis, M. (1990). *Liar's poker: searching through the wreckage of Wall Street*. New York: *Penguin Putnam, Inc.*
3. Burrough, B. & Helyar, J. (1992). *Barbarians at the gate*. New York: HarperPerennial.
4. Ashford, M. (1998). *Con tricks*. London: Simon & Schuster.
5. Weiss, A. (1995). *Our emperors have no clothes*. Franklin Lakes, NJ: Career Press.
6. Pinaults, L. (2000). *Consulting demons*. New York: Harper Collins.

These books provide the insider's perspective on how consulting firms can at times lead management at their clients to make decisions that are in their own best interests at the expense of what might truly be best for the client. At times humorous and at other times frightening, these eye-opening recitations of the techniques used by consultants to confuse, obfuscate, and manipulate clients against doing what they should in favor of what the consultant would prefer or stand to benefit the most from are clarion calls to all clients to retain control over their consulting projects, suppliers, and outcomes.

Magazines and Trade Journals

The following magazines might assist you in keeping current on what other business leaders are doing with consultants and which consultants are doing interesting projects:

1. *Business 2.0*, published by The FORTUNE Group at Time Inc., a Time Warner Company.
2. *Consulting Magazine*, published by Kennedy Information Inc.
3. *Fast Company*, published by Gruner and Jahr USA Publishing.
4. *Inc.*, published by Gruner and Jahr USA Publishing.
5. *Newsweek*, published by Newsweek Inc.
6. *TIME*, published by Time Inc., a Time Warner Company.

Additional Sources

In my consulting career, I have been approached by organizations offering to broker my services to clients for a fee. In exchange for providing opportunities for engagements, these "brokers" charge a percentage of the engagement fee to the client.

1. Connect4Training — www.connect4training.com
2. ProSavvy — www.prosavvy.com